The Mummy's Tale

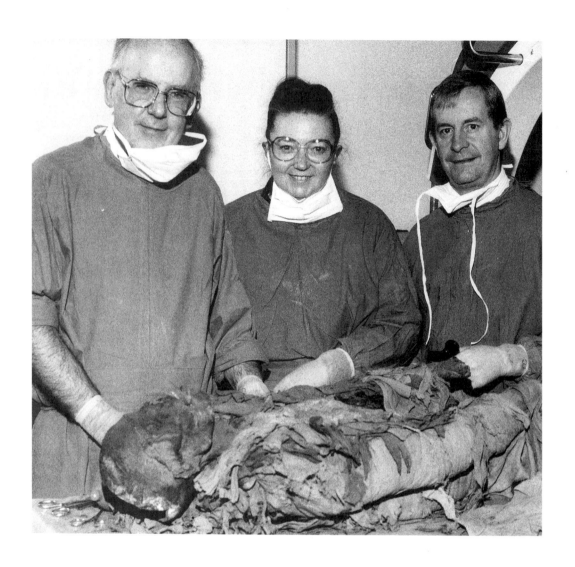

The Mummy's Tale

The Scientific and Medical Investigation of Natsef-Amun, Priest in the Temple at Karnak

Edited by

Dr A.R. David and Dr E. Tapp

St. Martin's Press
New York

Acknowledgments

As with all the research programmes undertaken by the Manchester Mummy Team, enthusiastic support has been given by the staff of museums and of various hospital and university departments. On this occasion, we owe a particular debt of gratitude to Roy Garner and Bill Hutchinson of the Manchester Museum, to the staff of the Leeds City Museum, the Preston Royal Hospital, the University Department of Radiology and the Medical Illustration Unit at the University of Manchester Medical School, and the University of Manchester Dental Hospital.

In the production of the book, we should like to thank Mr A.E. David; Mrs C.M. Higginbottom and Miss S. Ronan for their help in typing the manuscript; and Mr G. Thompson for photography. To our British publisher, Michael O'Mara Books Limited, we would like to record our appreciation, particularly to Michael O'Mara and Catherine Taylor.

In addition to this written account, the film made by Yorkshire Television provides a visual record of the Leeds Mummy investigation. We are grateful to Paul Dunstan, the producer, and his colleagues for their interest and involvement in our work, and to Bales Tours Ltd for facilities in Egypt.

Finally, the Manchester Team would like to express their thanks to Peter Brears, Director of the Leeds City Museums, for inviting them to undertake the examination of the Leeds Mummy, and for his encouragement and support throughout the project.

Rosalie David,
Manchester Museum.

Picture Acknowledgments

The line drawings on pages 112 and 114 (Figs. 40 and 42) are reproduced by kind permission of the artist, Hilary Wilson

The illustration on page 115 (Fig. 43) is reproduced by Courtesy of the Trustees of the British Museum

Frontispiece
Dr Edmund Tapp, Dr Rosalie David and Ken Wildsmith begin the 1990 autopsy of Natsef-Amun

Library of Congress Cataloging-in-Publication Data

David, A. Rosalie (Ann Rosalie)
    The mummy's tale : the scientific and medical investigation of Natsef-Amun, priest in the temple at Karnak / Rosalie David and Edmund Tapp.
        p.   cm.
    ISBN 0-312-09061-7
    1. Mummies—Egypt.   2. Natsef-Amun, d. ca. 1000 B.C.
3. Mummies—Radiography—England—Manchester.
4. Paleopathology—Egypt.   I. Tapp, Edmund.   II. Title.
DT62.M7D36   1993
932'.015'092—dc20   92-34389
                                                                   CIP

First Published in Great Britain by Michael O'Mara Books Limited.

First U.S. Edition: January 1993
10 9 8 7 6 5 4 3 2 1

Book design and maps: Simon Bell

Contents

Notes on Contributors

The following specialists, most of them members of the Manchester Mummy Team, contributed to this book:

Editors

A. Rosalie David, BA, Ph.D.
Director of the Manchester Egyptian Mummy Research Project since its inception in 1973. Took a degree in Egyptology at University College London and proceeded to a Ph.D. on religious ritual in ancient Egyptian temples at the University of Liverpool. Now Keeper of Egyptology with the status of Senior Lecturer in the Manchester University Museum. Also holds post of Honorary Lecturer in Comparative Religion in the University of Manchester. Author of 16 books on Egyptian history and religion, and editor of four previous books about the Mummy Project.

E. Tapp, MD, F.R.C.Path., MRCS(Eng), LRCP(Lond).
Qualified in medicine in 1959 and proceeded to an MD at Liverpool in 1964. Became a Member of the Royal College of Pathologists in 1968 and was awarded the Fellowship of the College in 1980. Has held posts in the University Departments of Pathology in both Liverpool and Manchester and is now Consultant in charge of the Departments of Histopathology and Morbid Anatomy at the Royal Preston Hospital and Clinical Director of the laboratories at the Royal Preston Hospital. Honorary Member of the Swedish Academy of Medical Science. He has been an active member of the Manchester Mummy team for 17 years, contributing to the four previous books published by the team and editing one of them jointly with Rosalie David.

The other contributors are listed alphabetically:

Miguel Aguirreburualde, FIMLS   Chief Medical Laboratory Scientist responsible for immunohistochemistry and electron microscopy within the Department of Histopathology at the Royal Preston Hospital.

Ruth Ashington   Superintendent Radiographer at the University of Manchester Dental Hospital. Has radiographed the mummies for the Manchester Project since 1974.

P.C.D. Brears, Dip.A.D., FMA, FSA   Director of Leeds City Museums. Has written a number of books and articles on the history of museums and on individual specimens.

Angela Clayton, FIMLS Chief Medical Laboratory Scientific Officer in the Department of Neuropathology at the Royal Preston Hospital.

T. Flaherty, MB, B.Ch.(NUI), MRCP (UK), MRC Path. Qualified in medicine in Cork in 1972. Became a Member of the Royal College of Physicians in 1975 and a Member of the Royal College of Pathologists in 1979. Has held posts as Senior Registrar in Haematology in several Manchester hospitals and is now Consultant Haematologist at the Royal Preston Hospital.

T.J. Haigh, FIMLS Senior Chief Medical Laboratory Scientific Officer in charge of the Blood Transfusion Department at the Royal Preston Hospital.

Miss C.W. Hart Superintendent Radiographer, University Department of Diagnostic Radiology, University of Manchester.

Professor I. Isherwood, MD, FRCP, FRCR Professor of Diagnostic Radiology, University of Manchester.

Catherine Asher-McDade, BDS, FDSRCS, D.Orth.RCS Consultant Orthodontist, Bolton, Blackburn and University of Manchester Dental Hospital.

Judith Miller, BDS General Dental Practitioner in orthodontic practice in Manchester.

R.A.H. Neave, FMAA, AIMI Joined the University of Manchester in 1959 as Medical Artist. Currently holds the post of Artist in Medicine and Life Sciences in the University Department of Surgery, Manchester Royal Infirmary and the Department of Cell and Structural Biology, University of Manchester. Has reconstructed heads for both forensic and archaeological purposes since 1975.

G. Thomson Photographer at Manchester Museum and Official Photographer of the University of Manchester. Covered the current project and the unwrapping of Mummy 1770 in 1975.

Pamela Thompson, FIMLS Senior Chief Medical Laboratory Scientific Officer in charge of the Department of Neuropathology at the Royal Preston Hospital.

K. Wildsmith From an engineering background, moved into a sales career. Originally a Senior Salesman with KMI (KeyMed Industrial) selling remote visual inspection equipment, and now Product Manager with Nikon UK. Became closely involved in the Manchester Mummy Project after KMI was approached for assistance in examining various mummies with endoscopic equipment.

Introduction

A.R. David

In 1828 the members of the Leeds Philosophical and Literary Society undertook one of the earliest recorded scientific investigations of an Egyptian mummy. The team, which included a physician, a surgeon and a chemist, as well as the society's secretary, performed a partial unwrapping and dissection of the mummy, followed by a chemical analysis of parts of the mummy and an anatomical study, as well as a translation and interpretation of the associated hieroglyphic texts. The investigation was a model for its time and may rightly be regarded as a pioneering venture in this field. Details relating to the man's physical condition and the techniques of mummification were discovered; and from the inscriptional evidence it was deduced that the man had been a priest named Natsef-Amun who served in the great Karnak temple complex at Thebes in Upper Egypt.

The 1828 investigation, although competent, naturally reflected the limitations of the day, and when, in 1989, P. C. Brears, the Director of the Leeds City Museum, invited Dr Rosalie David and the members of the Manchester Egyptian Mummy Research Project to undertake a new scientific study of Natsef-Amun's mummy, they welcomed this opportunity to compare techniques available in the early nineteenth century with those in use today. This book tells the story of that investigation and how the use of conventional radiology, computed tomography (CT) scans, endoscopy and histology, serology and dental studies can add to the existing knowledge of someone who has been dead for some three thousand years. A new autopsy was performed, this time using virtually non-destructive techniques, and a scientific facial reconstruction shows us how Natsef-Amun would have appeared to his contemporaries, before his physical remains were shrivelled by the mummification process.

This account of Natsef-Amun is something of a detective story: it illustrates how multidisciplinary scientific studies can give a picture of daily existence in ancient Egypt which is more realistic, but often less glamorous, than the view provided by art and literature. Natsef-Amun, well placed in society and with a successful career, participated in the sacred rituals offered to Egypt's greatest deities, but the investigation shows that he suffered sickness and disease and possibly endured a violent death.

The study of ancient Egyptian human remains holds out unique opportunities. Relatively large numbers of mummified remains still survive, partly because the near-ideal environmental conditions have preserved the bodies, and partly because the ancient Egyptian religious beliefs prompted the development of mummification and its continuation over a period of some three thousand years. Egypt also has a relatively unbroken population sequence, particularly in the more remote regions of the Nile Valley which remained isolated to some extent from the later arrivals who settled mainly in the Delta. Thus, Egypt provides an unequalled opportunity to study disease in a society which has remained fairly constant and has survived in a virtually unchanged environment for thousands of years.

1 Early Investigations of Mummies

A.R. David

Dr Margaret Murray, a pioneer in the field of Egyptian palaeo-pathology, wrote in 1910:

> Archaeology has been raised to the rank of a science within one generation: before that it was merely the pastime of the dilettante and the amateur who amused himself by adding beautiful specimens to his collection of ancient art . . . Then came the period of the enthusiast in languages, to whom inscriptions were the joy of life. And now there has arisen a new school to whom archaeology is a science, a science which embraces the whole field of human activity.
>
> (Murray, 1910)

The Battle of Waterloo (1815) marked the end of the Napoleonic Wars and ushered in a period of great change; distant lands such as Egypt became accessible to European travellers, and interest in the ancient Egyptian civilization grew rapidly. Museums in Europe and Britain were established by those who were interested in ancient cultures, and mummies and other artefacts were eagerly sought for these collections. Indeed, mummies had aroused antiquarian interest from the seventeenth century AD but in earlier times they were sought for quite different reasons.

In 1658, Sir Thomas Browne, the philosopher, wrote, 'Mummy is become Merchandise, Mizraim cures Wounds and Pharaoh is sold for Balsams', and as early as AD 1100 (and probably before), doctors had been prescribing 'mummy' for their patients. This custom was established first in Alexandria, and the preserved bodies of ancient Egypt were apparently credited with the same healing properties as *mumia*, the natural bituminous exudation found on the Mummy Mountain in Persia (see page 37). The Arab historian Abd' al-Latif comments on this: 'The mummy found in the hollows of corpses in Egypt differs but immaterially from the nature of mineral mummy; and where any difficulty arises in procuring the latter, may be substituted in its stead' (Fagan, 1975).

Mummy was soon widely used, and in the sixteenth and seventeenth centuries it became one of the most commonly prescribed drugs. Many physicians held it in high regard, but at least one writer – Ambrose Parey – could say nothing in its favour: 'This wicked kinde of drugge, doth nothing help the diseased . . . it also inferred many troublesome symptomes, as the paine of the heart or stomacke, vomiting, and stinke of the mouth' (Parey, 1634). Nevertheless, apothecaries' shops throughout Europe sold it as an expensive and effective medicine, and it was recommended for such diverse ailments as bruises, wounds, abscesses, fractures, concussions, paralysis, epilepsy, coughs, nausea, ulcers and other conditions. It was frequently mixed with herbs to make it more palatable for the patient.

The law of supply and demand had ensured that a flourishing trade in mummy developed from the outset; as Thomas Pettigrew, a nineteenth-century surgeon, commented, 'No sooner was it credited that mummy constituted an article of value in the practice of medicine than many speculators embarked in the trade; the tombs were sacked, and as many mummies as could be obtained were broken into pieces for the purpose of sale' (Pettigrew, 1834).

Large profits were to be made, and many foreign merchants were soon trading in this commodity. Mummies or fragments, made into packages in Cairo or Alexandria, were brought to Europe. Attempts by the Egyptian authorities to limit the export of this material simply led to a greater demand and, when ancient mummified tissue could not be obtained in sufficient quantities, other measures were introduced. Guy de la Fonteine of Navarre, investigating the trade in Alexandria in 1564, discovered that genuine mummified tissue was being simulated by exposing to the sun the bodies of the recently dead (often those of executed criminals). This desiccated the body tissues which could then be exported as 'mummy'. Eventually, stern measures were introduced by the Egyptian government to reduce the export of mummies; their removal from Egypt became illegal and substantial taxes were imposed on the dealers. Nevertheless, some continued to trade, and mummy achieved widespread and even royal approval: King Francis I of France is said to have carried with him on all occasions some powdered mummy mixed with pulverized rhubarb, to treat his ailments, and mummy remained a popular medicinal ingredient until the early nineteenth century.

Once mummies began to attract antiquarian interest and to be regarded as collectable curiosities by museums and private individuals, a new type of dealer emerged. These men 'excavated' in Egypt and acquired antiquities which they then sold to major collectors. One particularly successful individual was Giovanni Belzoni (1778–1823), an Italian excavator, explorer and adventurer who originally went to Egypt as a hydraulics expert. When this venture failed, he entered the employ of Henry Salt, the British Consul-General in Egypt, to remove large statuary which would eventually come to form part of the British Museum's collection in London. Belzoni visited many sites in Egypt, and discovered six royal tombs at Thebes, his most important find being the tomb of Sethos I in the Valley of the Kings; Belzoni, his wife Sarah, and their man-servant copied the magnificent wall scenes in this tomb with considerable skill, and their original sketches and watercolours are now in the Bristol Museum, England.

Belzoni's methods of excavation were sometimes unorthodox, although they were not radically different from those of his contemporaries. One one occasion, at Qurneh (on the west bank opposite the modern town of Luxor), he paid a regular wage and bonuses to tomb robbers, so that he could acquire as many mummies as possible in a short time. In his own account of excavating, he gives a vivid description of his ordeal in entering one tomb:

> After getting through those passages, some of them two or three hundred yards long, you generally find a more commodious place, perhaps high enough to sit. But what a place of rest: surrounded by bodies, by heaps of mummies in all directions, which, previous to my being accustomed to the sight, impressed me with horror . . . though, fortunately, I am destitute of the sense of smelling, I could taste that the mummies were rather unpleasant to swallow.

(Belzoni, 1821)

Fig. 1 (overleaf)
Excavations in Egypt in the nineteenth century. After the time of Napoleon, there were many 'digs' in Egypt, with archaeologists seeking out antiquities for museums and private collectors in Europe and America

On 21 May 1821, Belzoni held an exhibition of some of his discoveries at the Egyptian Hall in Piccadilly, London. These included a model, over fifty feet long, of the tomb of Sethos I, his greatest discovery, as well as two full-scale reproductions of chambers in this tomb. The exhibition was a great success and continued until 1822; before it opened to the public, a mummy of a young man was unwrapped before an invited audience of eminent doctors. Such spectacles were to become popular during this period, when increasing numbers of

13

European travellers were spending a winter vacation in Egypt and returning home with exotic souvenirs. In 1833, the monk Father Géramb commented to the Egyptian ruler, Mohammed Ali Pasha, 'It would be hardly respectable, on one's return from Egypt, to present oneself in Europe without a mummy in one hand and a crocodile in the other.'

Amelia B. Edwards' book *A Thousand Miles up the Nile* (1877) also affirmed that 'There is, in fact, a growing passion for mummies among Nile travellers' (Edwards, 1877) and the demand became so great that prices rose accordingly, making it a 'costly luxury' to acquire a mummy.

Once these souvenirs had been brought home, some of the mummies were unwrapped or 'unrolled' before invited audiences. These were social events, the highlight of many an At Home, but they had little scientific value; no detailed notes were taken and the important information which could have been derived from them was irretrievably lost. However, there were also some serious investigations during this period, such as the Leeds autopsy in 1828, and Belzoni's spectacular unrollings, although of little scientific value, served to inspire a man who was to make a major contribution in this field.

Thomas Joseph Pettigrew (1791–1865), an Englishman and naval surgeon's son, was born in London; he followed his father's profession, practising in Savile Row, and was a man of wide interests, participating in most of the literary and archaeological developments of his day. A meeting with Belzoni in 1818 inspired his interest in Egyptology and persuaded him to take up the study of Egyptian hieroglyphs. He acknowledges his indebtedness to Belzoni in the introduction to his book *A History of Egyptian Mummies and an Account of the Worship and Embalming of Sacred Animals* (1834) where he states: 'I had the gratification of knowing the lamented Belzoni, that most intrepid and enterprising traveller, and by his kindness, I was present at the opening of three mummies'.

With his surgeon's training, it is understandable that Pettigrew's main contribution would relate to mummification and the diseases of the ancient Egyptians, and he unrolled and gave demonstrations on a number of mummies. He purchased some of these for his own collection of Egyptian antiquities, but others were presented to him by friends and colleagues so that he could autopsy them. The unrollings and investigations were performed at various London venues, in the presence of titled, medical, literary and scientific audiences. His book, later described as 'a monument of exact observation' (Smith and Dawson, 1924), gave an account of his examination of several mummies, and commented on the development and significance of mummification. The procedure adopted at each unwrapping is

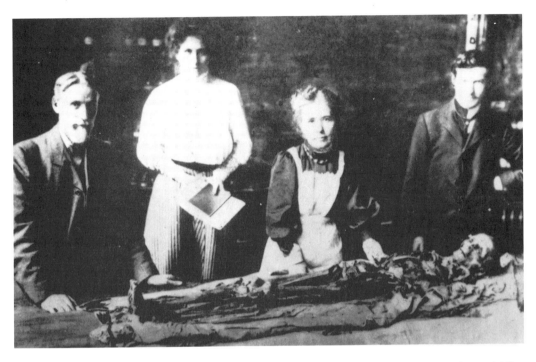

Fig. 2 *Dr Margaret Murray and her colleagues unwrapping the mummy of one of the Two Brothers in the Chemical Theatre at the University of Manchester in 1908. The mummies had been discovered, together with their coffins and funerary goods, in a previously undisturbed tomb at Der Rifeh in Middle Egypt*

detailed; as with the Leeds autopsy, Pettigrew used a multidisciplinary approach, consulting experts who could comment on the textile fibres of the bandages and identify the insects found in the mummies.

Another Savile Row medical practitioner who pursued the investigation of mummified remains was Augustus Bozzi Granville (1783–1872). Italian in origin, Granville had spent time early in his life as a political prisoner; on his release, he left Italy and travelled in the East before eventually taking up residence in London, where he assumed the name of Granville. Like Pettigrew, his interest in Egyptology led him to undertake scientific studies and in 1825 he published an account of his investigation of an Egyptian mummy of the Persian Period which showed evidence of ovarian disease (Granville, 1825).

Such studies gave the examination of mummies a scientific basis and laid the foundation for future research. However, the general enthusiasm for the frivolous pursuit of unrolling mummies waned, to be replaced by a more censorious attitude towards any investigation of the long-since dead. It was not until 1908 that serious interest in this type of research was revived when, in Manchester, Dr Margaret Murray unwrapped and autopsied the mummies of two brothers, using multidisciplinary medical, scientific and archaeological studies to gain as much information as possible about the tomb, funerary possessions, and bodies of the two men. At that time, she felt it necessary to justify the opening of tombs and the examination of human remains in terms of the new knowledge that could be gained, claiming that 'every vestige of ancient remains must be carefully studied and recorded without sentimentality and without fear of the outcry of the ignorant' (Murray, 1910).

Elsewhere, other pioneers were advancing the new science of Egyptian palaeopathology. In Cairo, Grafton Elliot Smith held the Chair of Anatomy at the Government School of Medicine. His early work in this field was carried out in 1901 on a series of ancient Egyptian bodies found in Upper Egypt; their bone measurements were recorded and the mummification procedures were examined. Another project involved the rescue and autopsy of some six thousand mummies; this resulted from the alterations which were carried out from 1900 on the dam at Aswan and which, with the consequent rise in water levels, would have ensured the destruction of many mummies in the area. Elliot Smith, with the aid of two specialists (W. R. Dawson and F. W. Jones) sent out specially from England, directed the examination of the mummies and was able to reveal for the first time many of the diseases which had afflicted the ancient Egyptians.

When the royal mummies of the New Kingdom were discovered Elliot Smith carried out an extensive examination of them which enabled him to compile a history of the development of techniques used in mummification. This formed the basis of his book (with co-author Warren Dawson) entitled *Egyptian Mummies* (1924); his study of the human remains of the kings and queens was published as the classic work *The Royal Mummies* (1912). When the tomb of the 18th Dynasty pharaoh Tuthmosis IV was discovered, complete with the king's body, in 1903, the mummy was taken to Cairo and unwrapped in public prior to a detailed investigation which was carried out in private by Elliot Smith. The examination was significant as the first time that radiography was used for the study of a royal mummy.

In the early years of the twentieth century, other pioneers were producing important results. Armand Ruffer, Professor of Bacteriology at Cairo's Government School of Medicine, began his investigation of the traces of disease in Egyptian mummies and skeletons, and laid the foundations for the study of histopathology in relation to Egyptian human remains. In a series of successful experiments, he developed methods of rehydrating ancient tissues so that they resumed something of their original condition, and this enabled him to examine them histologically to determine evidence of disease (see Chapter 10). His articles on the subject were collected and published after his death as *Studies in the Palaeopathology of Egypt* (Moodie, 1921).

The third man who contributed greatly in the scientific field was also based in Cairo. Alfred Lucas (1867–1945), an Englishman, initially went to Egypt because he suffered from lung trouble. There, he held a number of posts, including Chemist to the Antiquities Service from 1923 to 1932. His scientific background enabled him to undertake the analyses of many ancient materials and substances, and to advise on the restoration and consolidation of antiquities such as those found in the tomb of Tutankhamun at Thebes and in the royal tombs at Tanis. He was the author of more than sixty-five works, but perhaps his most significant book was *Ancient Egyptian Materials and Industries*, which was published in 1926. This gives an account of his analyses, carried out over many years, of the materials used by the ancient Egyptians; it remains a fundamental study, and his experiments regarding mummification techniques were the first to show that most of the Classical writer Herodotus' account of these techniques was accurate but that dry natron rather than immersion in a natron solution had almost certainly been the method used by the Egyptians (see page 46).

Investigations and studies carried out in the nineteenth and early twentieth centuries formed the basis of more recent research which has gained momentum again over the past twenty-five years. The introduction of virtually non-destructive techniques to examine mummies has allowed palaeopathologists to gain maximum information with minimal damage to the bodies, and the results add considerably to our understanding of life in ancient Egypt. Indeed, the argument in favour of continuing research is particularly well expressed by William Flinders Petrie, the so-called 'Father of British Egyptology', who stated:

> To raid the whole of past ages, and put all that we think effective into museums is only to ensure that such things will perish in the course of time. A museum is only a temporary place. There is not one storehouse in the world that has lasted a couple of thousand years . . . It is then to the written record and the published illustrations that the future will have mainly to look.
>
> (Petrie, 1904)

2   The Geography and History of Ancient Egypt

A.R. David

The Geography of Egypt

The historical development of every civilization is moulded to some extent by geographical and environmental factors, but ancient Egypt was more dependent than most upon the regularity of natural phenomena; with a negligible rainfall, the country is, and always has been, in the words of the oft-quoted Classical writer Hecateus, the 'gift of the Nile'. This great river, Africa's longest, rises three degrees south of the equator in the region of the Great Lakes. As the White Nile, it is joined at Khartoum by the Blue Nile. Between Khartoum and Aswan, the river is interrupted by six cataracts which take the form of scattered and irregular piles of rock in the river's course; these hamper navigation, particularly at the Fourth, Second and First Cataracts. The First Cataract is situated just south of Aswan (where the ancient town of Elephantine was established) and thereafter the Nile flows on its uninterrupted course for some six hundred miles to the Delta. Fanning out through this low plain, it finally passes, through two main branches at Rosetta in the west and Damietta in the east, into the Mediterranean.

The total territory of Egypt is extensive, but most of it is desert, so that the main centres of population developed along the Nile Valley and in the Delta. Compared with other ancient civilizations in the Near East, Egypt occupied an enviably secluded location in Africa; natural barriers effectively protected

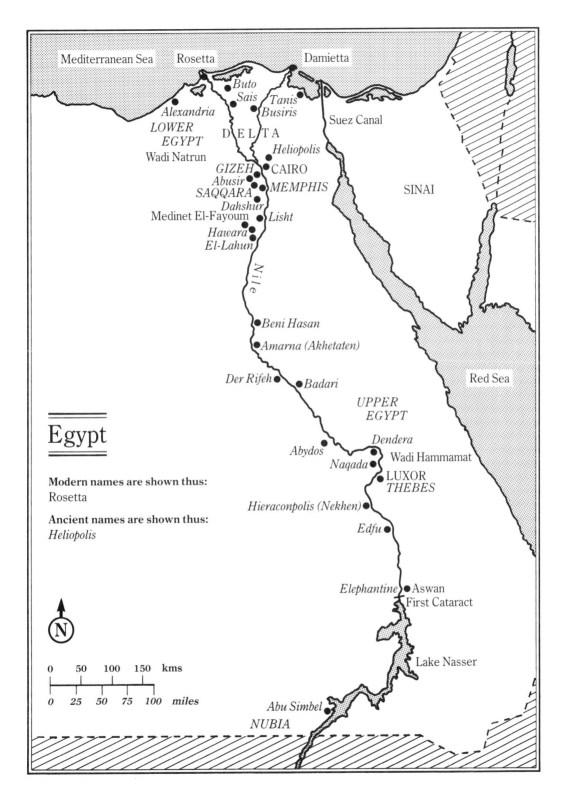

Mediterranean Sea   Rosetta   Damietta

Buto
Sais   *Tanis*
Busiris
Alexandria   Suez Canal
LOWER   D E L T A
EGYPT
Wadi Natrun   *Heliopolis*

GIZEH ● CAIRO   SINAI
Abusir
SAQQARA   *MEMPHIS*
Dahshur
Medinet El-Fayoum   *Lisht*
Hawara
El-Lahun

Nile

●*Beni Hasan*

●*Amarna (Akhetaten)*

Der Rifeh ●   ●*Badari*

UPPER
EGYPT   Red Sea

Dendera
Abydos ●   Wadi Hammamat
Naqada
Egypt   LUXOR
                                 THEBES

Hieraconpolis (Nekhen) ●

Modern names are shown thus:
Rosetta   *Edfu* ●

Ancient names are shown thus:
Heliopolis

                    Elephantine ● Aswan
                                 First Cataract

N

                                 Lake Nasser

0   50   100   150 kms

0   25   50   75   100 miles

                    Abu Simbel ●
NUBIA

the inhabitants against foreign invasion and outside intervention during the early and formative period of the civilization. The people were able to develop distinctive art forms, architecture, religious beliefs and customs, and a unique social structure, on which later direct contact with other peoples had minimal effect.

The physical barriers were formidable: to the north lay the Mediterranean which effectively deterred invasion, although it enabled the Egyptians to establish early trading contacts with other lands. On the east, the Red Sea provided another protection, and the region between this sea and the Nile Valley – the Eastern Desert – was the home of nomads. To the west there lay another inhospitable area – the Libyan or Western Desert, with its scattering of oases. The Egyptians had always had contact with the Libyan tribes and had traded with them, but until later times they posed no threat to Egypt's security. Away to the south was the ancient land of Nubia (which occupied the southern and northern areas respectively of the modern states of Egypt and the Sudan).

Nubia was rich in gold and granite, both commodities highly prized by the Egyptians. Consequently, from *c*.2900 BC the Egyptians pursued a policy of colonization in this area, to ensure their access to these materials. The Nubians later became completely 'Egyptianized' and posed no threat to their northern neighbour, although the Egyptian rulers were constantly vigilant in this area, leading military campaigns to subdue the local population and building fortresses along this frontier.

Hemmed in by such barriers, Egypt presented only one relatively easy route of access to determined invaders; this was in the north-east, across the northern part of the Sinai Peninsula, and early infiltrations probably entered the country from this direction.

In antiquity, the Egyptians called their country Kemet, which is translated as the Black Land. This referred to the rich black mud which successive inundations deposited on the riverbanks. The low annual rainfall (rain being an exceptional event in the south) was always insufficient to support crops and animals throughout the country, and the Egyptians have always had to rely on the annual inundation of the Nile in order to cultivate their land. Each year, the rains falling on the highlands of Ethiopia to the south increased the water in the river to such an extent that it rose and flooded its banks; the silt brought down by the waters was spread across the fields, fertilizing the soil and making it productive so that, with assiduous husbandry, the people could reap abundant crops.

The effect of the inundation was first visible in Egypt at Aswan (the First Cataract) in late June, and soon afterwards the muddy silt began to arrive; the flood swelled and, as it reached the level of the surrounding fields, the dykes were breached and the land was covered by water to a depth of several feet. The flood finally reached the north months later, at the end of September, and the waters then gradually receded, with the river reaching its lowest level in the following April, when the dry, cracked earth would again await the life-giving inundation. Since they were so dependent upon this phenomenon, the Egyptians always feared that it would not occur, and although this dread was never realized, the height of the inundation varied from year to year and brought its own problems: a Nile that was too high would flood the land, bringing destruction, loss of life, and the ruination of the crops, while a low Nile brought famine. The erratic nature of the inundation was a constant threat to the people's safety and prosperity, and in antiquity, the gods were revered and petitioned for their support in obtaining a 'good Nile'. The advent of modern technology has meant that dams could be constructed at certain points along the river, and this has enabled the volume of water to be held back and supplied as required for irrigation through a series of canals.

The Egyptians had recognized the need to take communal measures to control and regulate the Nile waters early in their history. At some time before 3100 BC they constructed a complex irrigation system: the land was divided by earth banks or dykes into compartments of varying sizes into which, when the river rose, the water could be introduced through canals. The water was held there until it had deposited its rich silt and, when the Nile had fallen, any remaining water was drained off from the land so that the ploughing and sowing of the crops could begin. The construction and maintenance of this irrigation system required organization and co-operation between the different communities along the river, and was a major factor in the early political unification of Egypt.

Fig. 3 *These present-day workmen are using an Archimedes screw to lift water from one irrigation canal to another at a higher level. As the name suggests, this method of raising water dates from the Greek period*

The fertile Black Land symbolized abundance and life to the ancient Egyptians, but immediately beyond the cultivation lay the desert, stretching away to the horizon. In some parts of the Nile Valley the cultivation stretches for several miles on either side of the river, and is in turn fringed by the desert, but in places there is virtually no cultivation, and the desert cliffs rise steeply alongside the river. The Egyptians called the desert the Red Land (they used the name Deshret from which our own word is derived), since this was the predominant colour of the rocks and sand. They feared it as a place of desolation, terror and death, where wild animals roamed and nomadic marauders might be encountered. The marked contrast between the cultivated land and the desert was never far from their minds, and it coloured and influenced some of their earliest and most enduring religious beliefs and customs.

Around them, the Egyptians observed cycles of continuity: each night the sun died and was reborn at dawn on the horizon, and every year the Nile inundation reinvigorated the parched land. It was not difficult to imagine that individual human experience also followed such patterns. The supposed cycle of life, death and rebirth became a firmly established belief and affected the treatment of a person's body after death. Care was taken to bury the body since the owner was believed to need it in his continued existence after death. However, there was so little cultivable land that it could only support the towns and villages, agriculture and animal husbandry and could not be sacrificed to accommodate the burial of the dead. The cemeteries were therefore located on the edges of the desert, where the hot, dry sand had the effect of preserving the corpses indefinitely, producing a form of natural mummification which was to have a profound impact on the development of funerary beliefs and customs.

The History of Egypt
c.3100 BC – 4th century AD

The history of dynastic Egypt covers a period from *c*.3100 BC to the conquest of the country by Alexander the Great in 332 BC. Prior to *c*.3100 BC in the time generally known today as the Predynastic Period (*c*.5000–*c*.3100 BC), the people laid the foundation for the subsequent great advances in politics, technology, religion and the arts. After Alexander the Great conquered Egypt, the country was ruled by a line of Macedonian Greeks who were descended from one of Alexander's generals (Ptolemy I). This dynasty ended with the famous queen,

Cleopatra VII, who failed to prevent the absorption of her country into the Roman Empire in 30 BC. After her death, Egypt became a Roman province.

The basis of our modern chronology of ancient Egypt follows the scheme set out by the priest Manetho (323–245 BC) who wrote a chronicle of the Egyptian kings (*c*.3100–332 BC), dividing his king list into thirty-one dynasties. Historians still retain these dynasties, but group them into a small number of periods, such as the Old Kingdom or First Intermediate Period. The Chronological Table (page 168) shows these main divisions, as well as the periods that preceded and succeeded the dynasties.

Egypt was divided geographically into the Black Land and the Red Land, but the country also separates naturally into a northern region (the Delta) and a southern part (the Nile Valley). These two regions have always had clearly defined differences which affected the country's history, but they are also interdependent, united by the life force of the Nile. The Nile Valley is essentially a corridor, some six hundred miles in length in Egypt, through which the river flows northwards, having cut its course here over the millennia; on the two riverbanks is the narrow band of cultivation, hemmed in by the desert. This southern area formed Upper Egypt. Lower Egypt lay in the north, where the Delta fanned out behind the ancient capital city of Memphis (near modern Cairo); this region was a vast, low-lying plain, some hundred miles in length and two hundred miles across, where the fertile silt was deposited by the river in its final stages before it reached the sea, and where abundant fruit and crops could be grown.

During the Palaeolithic Period (before 5000 BC), vast areas of the Delta were covered with papyrus swamps, and the Nile Valley was itself virtually uninhabitable: for three months of each year it was under the waters of the inundation, and otherwise it was covered by lush vegetation and fringed by marshes and swamps where the two symbolic plants of historic Egypt – the papyrus and the lotus – grew in profusion. At this time, Egypt teemed with wildlife: there were crocodiles, hippopotamuses and cobras, as well as the Sacred Ibis, and in the surrounding deserts, lions, leopards, ostriches, gazelles and other creatures flourished in large numbers. Gradually, however, the floor of the Nile Valley became drier, and many of the birds and animals moved further south (although they were retained thousands of years later in the mythology and symbolism of historic Egypt). During this period, the people who had lived on the desert spurs and hunted the prolific game began to move down into the valley and, once the inundation had receded, to cultivate the rich soil. Some time between 5000 and 4000 BC, the hunting forays became increasingly infrequent and farming developed in Egypt; in this Neolithic Period, people organized themselves into communities and began to grow grain and to domesticate animals.

Over the centuries, two loosely organized communities were established, one in Lower Egypt (the Delta) and the other in Upper Egypt (the Nile Valley); mixed farming was practised in both areas, and there was probably a general similarity of culture. From the excavated remains in Upper Egypt, it has been possible to establish a chronological sequence which leads up to the 1st Dynasty (*c*.3100 BC), when the country became unified under one ruler. Within this chronological sequence, the archaeologists have been able to determine specific periods which have been named Badarian, Naqada I and Naqada II, and it is evident that several important changes and developments emerged in the course of Naqada II. For example, there was increased contact with other areas of the Near East, and it is possible that developments that appear *c*.3400 BC (writing, monumental brick tombs, and great advances in the arts and crafts) may have been set in motion by the arrival in Egypt of a new group of people.

Whatever the cause of these changes, it is clear that, towards the end of Naqada II, there were two separate kingdoms established in Egypt; the northern one, in the Delta, was known as the Red Land (distinct from the geographical Red Land) while its southern counterpart in the Nile Valley was called the White Land. They shared many features of a common culture, but ultimately, the southern rulers conquered the northern kingdom and the two political entities were brought together in *c*.3100 BC by King Narmer (Menes), who became the first king of the 1st Dynasty. The unification marked the beginning of Egypt's history, but the dualistic origin of the country was always remembered and recalled in constant references to the Two Lands and, in the ruler's titles, to his role as King of Upper and Lower Egypt.

In the Archaic Period that followed, Narmer's descendants ruled a unified state; the political and social organization of the country was established and great advances were made in technology and building techniques. However, it was in the Old Kingdom (*c*.2686–*c*.2181 BC) that the civilization reached its first peak. Substantial mudbrick tombs had been introduced in earlier times for royalty and the nobility, to protect their bodies and tomb goods for use by their spirits in the afterlife. Today, these are known as mastaba tombs since the shape of the superstructure resembles the bench (Arabic word *mastaba*) which is placed outside houses in modern villages in Egypt. These mastabas were retained for the great nobles, although the mass of the population continued to be buried in shallow

Fig. 4 *The pyramid of Chephren at Gizeh. This is smaller than the Great Pyramid built by his father, Cheops, although they appear to be similar in height. In the foreground is a so-called 'queen's pyramid'. The exact function of these buildings is uncertain: they may have housed the king's viscera, removed during mummification*

graves in the sand, but in the 3rd Dynasty (*c*.2650 BC), the concept of the pyramid as the place of the king's burial was introduced. The pyramid was first built, in a stepped form, at Saqqara; it was designed for King Djoser by Imhotep, his vizier and architect, and formed the central feature of an elaborate and unique funerary complex. This earliest pyramid form was developed from the mastaba, and Djoser's structure had started as a mastaba, but the building was enlarged and extended several times and eventually a six-stepped pyramid was produced.

Djoser's pyramid was the first of a long series which were built for the rulers of the Old and Middle Kingdoms. Early in the 4th Dynasty (*c*.2600 BC), the transition was made (possibly for religious reasons) from the step to the true pyramid, and pyramid-building reached its zenith at Gizeh, with the funerary complexes of Cheops, Chephren and Mycerinus. Here, the three major pyramids formed the main feature of a vast necropolis which also incorporated the mastaba tombs of many of the contemporary courtiers. The pyramid form was probably closely associated with the cult of Re, the sun god, being intended to provide the dead king with access, by means of magic, to the heavens. By this time, the pyramid had become one element in a whole complex of buildings which also included a Valley Temple joined by a covered causeway to the king's Mortuary Temple. Small subsidiary pyramids were also associated with some complexes, although their exact function remains uncertain.

The construction and maintenance of the pyramids and the employment of staff to service them became an increasing drain on Egypt's economic resources, so that by the 5th Dynasty (*c*.2450 BC), there was a marked reduction in the size of the pyramids and the quality of their construction. The cult of the sun god had risen to unprecedented importance, and the kings now devoted most of their resources to constructing temples for this deity and his priesthood, at the expense of the royal pyramids. They now sought other means of ensuring their own eternity, having series of spells (known today as the Pyramid Texts) inscribed on the interior walls of the pyramids; these were intended to overcome all dangers and to ensure the king's passage to heaven.

The mastaba tombs of the nobility were lavishly equipped with articles of everyday use which might be required in the next life, and the interior walls were carved and painted with scenes (arranged in horizontal bands known as registers) that illustrate the world in which these people lived. The pyramids, tombs and temples were built mainly of stone, intended to last for eternity, whereas the houses and even the palaces were constructed of mudbrick and have consequently survived less well, but there is sufficient evidence to indicate that the lifestyle of the wealthiest in this society was elegant and luxurious.

The Old Kingdom, perhaps most noted for its pyramid-building, also achieved excellence in art and literature. One important type of literature, known as the Wisdom Literature or Instructions in Wisdom, provides a unique insight into the society's moral and ethical values. These instructions were taught to boys who would become senior officials, and they emphasized the rigid social hierarchy, but they also promoted the virtues of truthfulness, respect for elders, and the kindly treatment of those at the bottom of the 'social pyramid'.

In the Old Kingdom, a great gulf divided the king from his subjects; this sprang from the idea that each ruler was half-divine, being the offspring of the union between Re, the chief state god, and the previous king's Great Royal Wife. The king alone could hope for individual immortality, but his subjects could experience immortality vicariously, through the royal bounty. The king reigned supreme (although confined to certain actions through precedent) over the nobles (who were usually members of his own family), the state officials who manned the extensive bureaucracy, the craftsmen who supplied the goods for the tombs (and, secondary to this, for daily needs), and the peasants who, as the largest section of the population, grew the food for the whole society and provided the heavy labour for pyramid construction.

Given the great and continuing drain on royal resources, this society could not hope to survive, and by the 6th Dynasty (*c.*2300 BC), various political, economic, social and religious factors contributed to its downfall. This collapse was followed, during the First Intermediate Period, by a time of anarchy, when the centralized government disappeared and Egypt returned to the fragmented rule of the Predynastic Period when local leaders controlled their own districts and fought each other. Chaos ensued: the monuments were desecrated, and robbers ravaged the graves; poverty, famine and disease became widespread. Some of Egypt's most famous literary works are believed to reflect the horrific conditions of this period which would have been unimaginable in the halcyon days of the Old Kingdom.

Gradually, a semblance of order returned, and in the 11th Dynasty (*c.*2000 BC), the princes of Thebes, who carried the family name of Mentuhotep, were able to restore some unity. Nebhepetre Mentuhotep was sufficiently powerful to build a unique funerary temple at Deir el Bahri, Thebes, which incorporated a small pyramid, temple and burial chamber cut into the adjoining cliff. However, there was no centralization as in the Old Kingdom, when the mastaba tombs of the nobility clustered at the base of the king's pyramid, and the craftsmen were no longer concentrated at Memphis. Local rulers, even if admitting the overlordship of the Mentuhoteps, now chose to be buried near to where they had lived, preparing tombs cut deep into the cliffs which were decorated by local artisans. Here, as in the mastaba tombs, the interior walls have lively painted scenes which show many aspects of daily life, and a whole range of locally produced funerary goods were buried with the owner.

With the advent of the Middle Kingdom (1991–1786 BC), Egypt again enjoyed a period of great prosperity under firm, centralized rule. The founder of the 12th Dynasty was Ammenemes I, a commoner who had usurped the throne. He and his descendants were dynamic and competent kings. The capital was moved north from Thebes to It-towy, and the practice of pyramid-building on conventional lines was revived. Various political innovations were introduced, to stabilize the kingdom and underpin centralized government: co-regency – when the king associated his chosen heir with him upon the throne – now became customary, and ensured a smooth succession on the king's death; and Sesostris III took measures (which are still unknown) to rid Egypt of the great provincial nobles so that they could never again jeopardize the king's supremacy as they had at the end of the Old Kingdom. No effective solution was ever found to limit the power of the priesthood, the other major threat to the king.

Despite the success of the Middle Kingdom rulers, different attitudes to the king's role had emerged after the collapse of the Old Kingdom. The royal patron deity, Re, never recovered his supreme status in the pantheon, and another god, Osiris, now gained widespread support: he could promise immortality to all his followers, rich or poor, if they could demonstrate exemplary lives. The afterlife now became universally available to the pious and was no longer dependent upon the royal bounty. This democratic attitude profoundly affected religious beliefs and brought about widespread changes in funerary customs.

Although the kings chose to be buried in pyramids, the nobles and officials could be buried in mastabas near the royal tomb or in rock-cut tombs. Many wealthy provincial nobles chose the rock-cut tombs in their own localities, extending a custom which had begun towards the end of the Old Kingdom. Cut into the cliffs along the Nile, these tombs each consisted of a decorated pillared hall and a burial chamber.

Sculpture, jewellery, art and literature of the time all reflect a period of wealth and stability, and Egypt also pursued a new dynamism in her foreign policy. Control over Nubia had lapsed in the First Intermediate Period (c.2181–1991 BC), and a new and more aggressive group of people had entered the area; a more forceful approach was now required, and Egypt regained Nubia, building a string of fortresses which they garrisoned to subdue any further uprising.

To the north, however, their policy was very different, and here they re-opened trading contacts with the Aegean islanders and the people of Byblos on the Syrian coast. Away to the east, on the Red Sea coast, they also fostered friendly relations with the land of Punt which supplied Egypt with incense.

However, prestige abroad and political stability at home were not to last. The Second Intermediate Period (c.1786–1567 BC) was again a time of decline with a breakdown in centralized control. Of the five dynasties which comprise this period, some had lines of native rulers who, in some cases, were contemporary, controlling different parts of the country. However, the 15th (1674–1567 BC) and 16th (c.1684–1567 BC) Dynasties were made up of foreign kings who had entered Egypt and established themselves, first settling in the Delta and then gradually extending their influence over much of Egypt. Manetho, the compiler of the king list, called them the Hyksos, and they were probably of Asiatic origin, although the exact location of their homeland (and their ethnic composition) has been much discussed.

The end of Hyksos domination and of the Second Intermediate Period was brought about by the native princes of the 17th Dynasty (c.1600 BC) who ruled at Thebes. They drove the Hyksos from Egypt, pursuing them into southern Palestine, and then claimed authority over the whole of Egypt, one of their number – Amosis I – establishing the 18th Dynasty (1567–1320 BC) and founding the New Kingdom.

The Hyksos intrusion had radically affected the Egyptian attitude regarding foreign policy. Before this time, although they had colonized Nubia, they had shown little interest in fighting their neighbours elsewhere, and gained the commodities they required through trading ventures. The advent of the Hyksos, however, demonstrated vividly to the Egyptians that others coveted their country and, whenever internal dissension occurred, would take the opportunity to invade. To prevent such attacks in the future, the Egyptians began to adopt an aggressive and expansionist foreign policy. During the 18th Dynasty, the kings (particularly Tuthmosis I, Tuthmosis III and Amenophis II) led a series of successful military campaigns to Palestine, Syria and Asia Minor. Their aim was to bring under Egyptian influence and control the petty independent states in Palestine, so as to prevent any serious attack being launched against Egypt from that direction. However, their policy brought them into conflict with Mitanni, the other great local power. This conflict was later resolved when it became evident that neither state would emerge as the complete victor: Egypt and Mitanni abandoned their differences and became friends and allies. However, Egypt subsequently faced a new rival, the Hittites, and in the 19th Dynasty (*c*.1250 BC), when Egypt renewed its claims in Syria and Palestine, kings Sethos I and Ramesses II campaigned vigorously against the new enemy. Ultimately, the combatants once again acknowledged stalemate and the conflict was resolved by a diplomatic alliance which was marked by the marriage of Ramesses II to a Hittite princess.

During that period of the 18th Dynasty when Egypt succeeded in establishing direct control over the petty states in Palestine, the first empire was created. Egypt was supreme over an area that stretched from the River Euphrates in the north to Nubia in the south, and succeeded in ruling effectively and benignly a disparate collection of states. Rather than impose direct rule, the Egyptians allowed the native princes, provided they were loyal to Egypt, to remain as rulers of their own cities and minor states, linking them together in a loose confederation. The states gave allegiance and tribute, and as long as Egypt remained strong the system worked well; but when the kings neglected their empire, these vassal princes would fall prey to the other ambitious powers in the area. Nevertheless, despite its shortcomings, and although the later empires of the Assyrians, Persians, Greeks and Romans were larger and more rigidly organized, the Egyptian Empire brought some degree of stability and cohesion to the area.

One result of Egypt's foreign policy was that its own wealth was substantially increased, both by the tribute paid by the vassal states and by the booty brought back from military campaigns. The main recipient of this wealth was the Theban god Amun and, particularly, the priesthood at his principal shrine, the Temple of Karnak at Thebes. Amun had been the local god of the Theban princes of the 17th Dynasty; their descendants, the founders of the 18th Dynasty, made him the supreme deity of the state pantheon, and when their campaigns gave Egypt its empire, Amun became the principal deity of all Egypt's possessions. Amun had been united with the old solar god Re, to eclipse any possible rivalry and to enhance his power and status; now known as Amen-Re, the god's priesthood at Thebes achieved unprecedented importance. By the middle of the 18th Dynasty, they claimed the right to select and support a particular candidate for the throne, if there was a disputed succession, declaring that this was the 'god's choice'. In building up the power and prestige of their old local god, the kings of this dynasty had effectively created a situation where their own position was threatened.

The god's cult centre of Thebes was now the state capital of Egypt and its empire, as well as being the country's religious capital. The kings had their official residence there and opposite this great city, on the west bank of the river, they selected a new burial site, known today as the Valley of the Kings. It was decided to abandon the pyramid for royal burials, since experience had taught them that such a structure would be readily identified as a treasure-house and rapidly plundered by tomb robbers; they now chose a remote and barren valley in the Theban hills. Here, rock-cut tombs were constructed for the kings of the 18th, 19th and 20th Dynasties, in the vain hope of defeating the tomb robbers.

The tombs were excavated into the mountainside (the deepest descends for over three hundred feet), and had a series of chambers and descending passages which were intended to defeat the plunderers. Although no two tombs are identical, they have a similar layout and decoration: the interior walls are sculpted or painted with scenes and texts which are taken from the funerary books (themselves ultimately derived from the Pyramid Texts of the Old Kingdom). These illustrate the king's journey through the underworld and were designed to give him magical protection and assist him through the multitude of dangers that lurked there and could hamper his passage. Not far away was the Valley of the Queens, where some of the royal wives and princes were buried in rock-cut tombs which were also decorated with scenes that showed the royal owners in the presence of the gods. Royal courtiers and officials had their rock-cut tombs excavated across this area, but here the wall scenes are different; they do not show the passage into the underworld but, as in earlier periods, vividly represent the daily activities of the owner so that he could perpetuate and enjoy his lifestyle in the next world.

Fig. 5 *Lotus columns in the Temple of Amun at Karnak. Such plant-form columns are found in most Egyptian temples; they represented the fertile landscape of the mythological island where creation was believed to have taken place*

Despite the elaborate precautions, the plundering of the tombs continued. Of the sixty or so tombs known in the Valley, only that of Tutankhamun (a minor king) has survived almost intact, and even that had been entered and partially robbed in antiquity. Many of the royal mummies, ravaged by the robbers searching for jewellery, were later rescued and reburied by the priests of the 21st Dynasty, in an attempt to protect them from further desecration (see pages 55–56).

Once the royal tombs were located in the narrow confines of the Valley of the Kings, there was no room to build a mortuary temple adjacent to the tomb, as had been done in the pyramid complexes. These temples – used for the burial ceremony and the perpetual offerings presented to ensure the king's continuation as a Royal Ancestor – were now constructed on the cultivated plain which lay on the west bank between the Valley and the river. Today, the magnificent temples of Hatshepsut at Deir el Bahri, of Ramesses II (the Ramesseum), and of Ramesses III at Medinet Habu are still relatively well-preserved examples of such foundations.

Towards the end of the 18th Dynasty, Amen-Re's priesthood wielded sufficient power to threaten the king himself, and several rulers began to take measures to counteract this. The traditional dynastic marriage had been between the Great Royal Daughter (the eldest daughter of the previous king and his chief queen) and the heir presumptive. The line of inheritance was thus deemed to pass through the female line, although the kingship was usually exercized by a man, and the 18th Dynasty had been more assiduous than most in preserving the role of the consanguineous marriage. However, by allowing the priests of Amen-Re to approve the person who would marry the Great Royal Daughter and thus inherit the throne, they were given undue influence over the succession. Perhaps to curtail this power, Tuthmosis IV and his son Amenophis III both took as their chief queens women who were not Great Royal Daughters. The son of Amenophis III, Amenophis IV (Akhenaten), was even more radical; not only did he take a non-royal queen, but he introduced reforms which involved the promotion of a monotheistic cult centred on the Aten (sun's disc), and he closed the temples of the other gods and disbanded their priesthood. The capital city was moved to Akhetaten (Amarna), and during this time of upheaval his queen, Nefertiti, and their elder daughters played significant political and religious roles. However, this 'revolution' was doomed to failure, since it had no general support; following the reigns of Tutankhamun (Akhenaten's son-in-law) and Ay (an elderly courtier), the throne passed to an army man, Horemheb, who masterminded the counter measures that restored traditional beliefs.

In the 19th Dynasty (*c*.1250 BC), the great kings Sethos I and Ramesses II reasserted Egypt's military power in Syria and Palestine, but soon there was a new threat on the western front where Libyan tribes were now attempting to infiltrate and settle. Later, they were joined in this by the Sea-peoples, a motley collection of itinerants from the north who were attracted by the fertile Delta. In the 19th and 20th Dynasties, under Merneptah and Ramesses III, the Egyptians faced and repelled these attacks, although ultimately the descendants of these Libyan tribesmen would become the rulers of the 22nd Dynasty (*c*.900 BC).

In relatively recent times, scholars have adopted the term Third Intermediate Period for the years that encompass the 21st to 26th Dynasties (*c*.1089–525 BC), when Egypt's great days were at an end. Natsef-Amun probably lived during the 20th Dynasty, when the decline had already begun, but the 21st Dynasty witnessed the schism when the legitimate kings continued to rule in the north from the city of Tanis, while a succession of high priests of Amun (nominally still under the king's control) wielded almost absolute political power in Thebes and the surrounding district. There followed the 22nd (*c*.900 BC) and 23rd (*c*.800 BC) Dynasties, when the descendants of the Libyan tribesmen who had infiltrated the Delta and settled at Bubastis became the kings of Egypt. The 25th Dynasty (*c*.700 BC), which is sometimes called the Ethiopian Dynasty, consisted of rulers of foreign origin who came from the south, thus reversing briefly the old trend of the Egyptian colonization of Nubia, but they were eventually driven back to their homeland by the Assyrian invaders from the north, who subsequently made Egypt part of their empire. Egypt's long decline was only briefly halted in the Saite Period (26th Dynasty, *c*.600 BC), when a line of native kings ruled from Sais in the Delta and revived some of the ancient glories. In this dynasty there were strongly nationalistic trends and a high level of excellence in the arts and crafts, although these took their forms and inspiration from much earlier models.

The Late Period (525–332 BC) witnessed the final years of decline. In the 27th (*c*.500 BC) and 31st (*c*.340 BC) Dynasties, the country again fell under foreign domination, this time becoming part of the Persian Empire. Egypt began to play an increasingly small role in world events as the centres of influence moved elsewhere, and the dynastic era was finally brought to an end when Alexander the Great conquered the country in 332 BC. When this King of Macedon died, his empire was divided, and Egypt came into the possession of one of his generals, Ptolemy Lagus, who, as Ptolemy I Soter, declared himself the legitimate King of Egypt. He and his descendants ruled the country until 30 BC, and since twelve of these kings bore the name Ptolemy, this is often known as the Ptolemaic Period. During this time, many Greeks came to settle in Egypt, and, unlike the Assyrian and Persian dominations which had made little impact on Egypt's traditions and customs, the Hellenistic culture came to prevail. The Greek language, customs, legal system, and religion were officially introduced into Egypt and actively promoted. The native population continued to preserve their age-old language and traditions but the Greeks now dominated the country. The new capital city of Alexandria (founded on the Mediterranean coast by Alexander the Great) became a great centre of learning, and other Greek cities were built elsewhere in Egypt. Nevertheless, the Ptolemies continued to support the traditional state religion of Egypt, with its gods, temples and priesthood, and even built new temples in the authentic style. This they did to establish their divine right to rule Egypt as the Pharaohs had done, and to justify the heavy and excessive taxes which they now imposed. The semi-divine status they claimed as the 'legitimate' heirs to the throne was used to protect their actions, but unlike the native kings, they did not rule according to the principles of *Ma'at* (truth), bringing order and balance to the kingdom, and general dissatisfaction soon led to opposition and rioting amongst the native population.

The death of Cleopatra VII in 30 BC brought this dynasty to an end, and Egypt passed to the Romans, becoming the personal possession of its conqueror, Augustus, and a province of the Roman empire. Life remained unchanged for most people, however, or even worsened; many features of Ptolemaic rule were retained, including the administrative system, and further heavy taxation was imposed. The Roman emperors followed the example of the Ptolemaic kings, and supported the ancient state religion; they made additions to the temples and were shown in the wall scenes as the divine and legitimate pharaohs who had the authority from the gods to own the country and its resources, and to exact taxes. The living standards of the native population declined further, and in terms of political status Egypt was now merely regarded as a possession which produced grain for the rest of the Roman Empire. In the fourth century AD, when the empire was partitioned into east and west, Egypt passed under Byzantium. After the edict of Emperor Theodosius I, Christianity had become the official religion of the Roman Empire, and it spread rapidly in Egypt. However, when the Arab conquest in AD 641 brought the long period of Roman rule in Egypt to an end, Islam gradually became the state religion, although a substantial minority, known from the sixteenth century as Copts, continued to practise Christianity.

3 The History of Mummification

A.R. David

The term 'mummy' is generally used today to describe a naturally or artificially preserved body in which desiccation of the tissues has enabled it to resist putrefaction. Such examples have been discovered in a number of countries, although originally the word 'mummy' was reserved for the artificially preserved bodies of the ancient Egyptians.

There are different views about the origin of the word itself, although the most widely accepted opinion is that mummy is probably derived from the Persian or Arabic word *mumia*, meaning pitch or bitumen. Abd' al-Latif, an Arab physician and writer of the twelfth century AD, explains that *mumia* was a substance that flowed down from mountain tops and, mixing with the waters that carried it down, coagulated like mineral pitch. In Persia, the Mummy Mountain was famous for the black bituminous material that oozed from it, and this was credited with medicinal and healing properties. It came into vogue as a medicinal ingredient (see page 11), and achieved fame in the highest circles; for example, in 1809, the King of Persia presented the Queen of England with a gift of *mumia*. Because there was such a demand for this substance, alternative sources were sought; the preserved bodies of the ancient Egyptians, with their blackened appearance, were likened to the true *mumia* and came to be credited with similar properties, and this led to their use as a medicinal ingredient in medieval and later times. It is probable that the term *mumia* was adopted for these bodies and has survived in the word mummy.

Human remains, consisting of the skeleton and body tissues, can be preserved indefinitely in a number of ways. In some cases, this comes about because of natural circumstances. The major factors in this unintentional form of preservation are environmental conditions such as dryness provided by the sand in which the body is buried, heat or cold resulting from the climate, or the absence of air in the burial. These factors can occur either singly or in combination, and they produce varying degrees of preservation in countries such as Egypt, Peru, Aleutia and Alaska (Cockburn and Cockburn, 1980). In north-western Europe, another method of unintentional preservation by natural means is encountered (Glob, 1969). Here, bodies were buried in bogs which by chance produced the right conditions for preservation: there were raised bogs which were acid and contained peat moss (sphagnum) and this, with its compressed layers, prevented oxygen from reaching the underlying layers; there were fens which contained lime; and there were the transitional bogs.

Elsewhere, naturally occurring environmental factors which produced unintentional mummification were sometimes deliberately enhanced to encourage mummification. Sometimes, the body would be dried thoroughly, by making use of natural heat sources such as the sun, fire or candle heat; the body might be cured by smoke; in other examples, the bodily cavities were stuffed and the body was packed around with dry grass and other natural materials. Another aid to preservation was the placing of the body in a sealed environment, so that the natural desiccation process could continue.

A unique method of intentional preservation by natural means was practised in Japan in the eleventh and twelfth centuries AD, when some of the priests pursued a form of self-mummification (Sakurai and Ogata, 1980). This involved the reduction of the bodily intake of nutrition for a period of three years, by abstaining from the consumption of rice, barley, corn, millet and beans; the priest then surrounded his body with many large candles, so that it became heat-dried. Ultimately, he would die from starvation, and the body was interred in an underground stone chamber for three years; after exhumation, it was kept in a sealed environment for seventeen days, and finally it was heat-dried again, probably using candles.

Despite these often curious practices of unintentional preservation and of intentional preservation using natural means, true mummification can really only be identified as a method which is not only intentional but which also incorporates several sophisticated techniques, making use of chemical and other agents. Many years of experimentation would be required to perfect such methods, and the most convincing evidence of this type of preservation is provided by the ancient Egyptian mummies.

The artificial preservation of the corpse was practised in

Egypt from the Old Kingdom (*c*.2686–2181 BC) through to the Christian era, only ceasing with the introduction of Islam after the Arab conquest in AD 641. However, the practice would have originated much earlier, when the Egyptians first developed a religious awareness and began to inter their dead on the edges of the desert.

There are no extant written records from Egypt's predynastic era, but the archaeological remains confirm the presence of religious customs which emphasized the requirement to bury the dead, and to preserve the bodies in as lifelike a state as possible. Because of scarcity of cultivable land, the earliest method of disposal was to bury the corpses in the desert. Naked, and perhaps enclosed in a reed or skin mat, the body was placed in a shallow pit-grave in the sand, and the environmental conditions – the sun's heat and the dryness of the sand – combined to preserve the body indefinitely. The body tissues became desiccated before decomposition set in, and the body fluids were absorbed into the surrounding sand. Examples of such bodies can be seen in some museums; the skin and hair are often still present, and there is a remarkable degree of preservation, so that, although they cannot strictly be classified as mummies, these bodies undoubtedly inspired the Egyptians' later attempts to undertake artificial preservation. Although, in time, true mummification was developed and used for the wealthier sections of society, it was this early and natural procedure which continued for the burial of the poorer classes throughout the dynastic period.

Ancient Egyptian civilization was distinguished by a clearly defined belief in a human existence which continued after death, but this individual immortality was considered to be dependent in part on the preservation of the body in as lifelike a form as possible. The human personality was regarded as a complex entity, and some elements, such as the Ba (soul) and Ka (spirit), were considered to be immortal and to perpetuate the essence of the individual after death. The Ka would need to return to the tomb from time to time, where it gained sustenance on behalf of its owner from the food offerings placed there by the relatives or Ka priest. In order to perform this duty satisfactorily, the Ka was believed to enter the deceased's body which it then used to gain nourishment from the food. To enable this procedure to take place, it became essential that the body was carefully preserved and that it retained a sufficient likeness to the deceased for the Ka to be able to recognize it.

Such religious beliefs were probably established as early as the Archaic Period (*c*3100–2686 BC), but at the same time more sophisticated burial arrangements were being introduced. Deeper and more elaborate tombs were constructed for the royal family and the great nobles, in which the tomb was marked above ground with a bench-shaped superstructure while the burial was placed in an underground chamber, lined with wood or mudbrick. The body itself was often enclosed within a wooden coffin, and food, domestic and other possessions were placed in the tomb for the owner to use in the next life. Despite these advances, however, the main purpose of the tomb – to preserve the body – was less successful: unlike the predynastic burials, the body was now no longer immediately surrounded by the heat and dryness of the sand. Rapid decomposition of the body tissues became a serious problem because preservation of the corpse was a primary religious requirement, and alternative methods were now sought.

There was certainly a period of experimentation when the Egyptians tried to develop an artificial means of retaining the body. Such attempts go back at least until the 2nd Dynasty (*c*.2700 BC): some fifty years ago, the archaologist Quibell discovered human remains in a cemetery of that date at Saqqara (Smith and Dawson, 1924) and these provided evidence of what were probably early experiments in mummification. Between the outer bandages and the bones of a 'mummy', Quibell found a large mass of corroded linen which possibly indicates that some attempt had been made to use natron (the substance eventually employed successfully by the Egyptians) or some other agent as a preservative by applying it to the skin surface. Generally, in this period and in the early years of the Old Kingdom (*c*.2686–2181 BC), the experiments were unsuccessful. They included the 'stucco mummies', examples of which were discovered by the German and American archaeologists, Junker and Reisner: the bodies were first covered with fine linen and then enclosed in stucco plaster, special attention being given to careful representation of the body features, and particularly the head. Another good example from the Old Kingdom (probably the 5th Dynasty, *c*.2450 BC) was the body discovered at Medum by Petrie in 1891, which was later presented to the Royal College of Surgeons in London. Here, there had been some attempt to preserve the body tissues, but mainly they had relied on recreating the bodily form, replacing the earlier loose body cover with close-fitting bandages which emphasized the physical contours. The limbs were wrapped separately, and the facial features, breasts and genitalia were moulded in resin-soaked linen. Such realism was not sufficient, however, since the body continued to decompose under the bandages, and the end result was a skeleton enclosed in an elaborate moulded structure.

The first definitive evidence that true mummification had been successfully achieved comes at the start of the 4th Dynasty (*c*.2600 BC). Egyptian mummification involved two basic procedures – the evisceration of the body (although not all mummies underwent this process) and the treatment of the tissues with natron, as a dehydrating agent – and both are evident in the human remains of Queen Hetepheres, the mother of Cheops who built the Great Pyramid at Gizeh. The Queen's tomb was discovered near her son's pyramid, and the burial contained her viscera, which had been placed in a special chest (it is assumed that the body itself was missing because it had been destroyed by robbers in the Queen's original burial place; subsequently, Cheops buried his mother's remains in a more secure location near his own tomb). Analysis of the packets containing the viscera showed that they had been immersed in a dilute solution of natron, so both evisceration and treatment with a dehydrating agent were evidently in use, at least for members of the royal family, as early as the 4th Dynasty. Prevention of decomposition of the tissues had obviously replaced the earlier attempts to create a modelled likeness of the deceased.

In addition to evisceration and desiccation, the body might also be anointed with oils and unguents and, in some cases, coated with resin, but these were essentially cosmetic devices. In the long history of mummification, there were two further major innovations. From perhaps as early as the Middle Kingdom (*c*.1900 BC), the brain was removed, and this procedure became widespread from the New Kingdom (*c*.1450 BC) onwards; secondly, during the 21st Dynasty (*c*.1089–945 BC), certain refinements were introduced to restore the shrunken body to a plumper and more realistic appearance. This involved packing the neck, face and other areas with materials such as linen, sawdust, earth, sand and butter, which were inserted through incisions in the skin.

There is sufficient evidence to allow us to reconstruct the process of mummification with some degree of accuracy. Apart from the mummies themselves, some of the materials connected with the process have survived; because they had come into direct contact with the deceased's body, they acquired a certain sanctity and were sometimes placed inside the coffin or packed into jars and put in the tomb or buried in a nearby pit. There is also the literary evidence. No Egyptian account survives which gives details of the technical processes involved in mummification, and there are no ancient illustrations, although wall scenes in the tombs of Thoy (No. 23) and Amenemope (No. 41) at Thebes (Dawson, 1927) show some of the stages in the preparation of the bandaging and decorating of the mummy. However, these provide interesting details rather than an accurate sequence. Some Egyptian texts allude to religious concepts associated with mummification (as in the Pyramid Texts, the

Coffin Texts and the Book of the Dead), and others mention some of the rituals that accompanied the procedure, but the only available detailed descriptions of the techniques which were employed are given in two Classical authors, Herodotus and Diodorus Siculus.

Herodotus was a Greek historian who lived in the fifth century BC and who travelled in Egypt and described many facets of life in that country. He provides the most complete account of mummification, but minor variations and additions are provided in the work of Diodorus, who was writing in the first century BC, and some information is also supplied in other Classical authors. These cannot be regarded as entirely accurate sources, as they were probably based to some extent on hearsay (Herodotus doubtless received much of his information from the Egyptian priests he encountered on his travels), and these accounts were all written centuries after mummification had passed its peak. There would have been some variation in the techniques over three thousand years, and information acquired by a foreign visitor in the fifth century BC was not necessarily valid for the earlier periods.

However, it is evident that the basic principles of evisceration and dehydration remained constant, but that these were only used to full effect for the most expensive burials. Herodotus claims that three methods of mummification were available according to cost. The most expensive (which produced the best results) involved the removal of the brain and the viscera, and this was followed by the dehydration of the body, using natron; then the body was washed and wrapped in bandages fastened together with gum. In the second method, 'cedar oil' (probably impure oil of turpentine or pyroligneous acid containing admixed oil of turpentine and wood tar) was injected into the body *per anum*, and it was then treated with natron. The third and cheapest method involved the injection of an unspecified liquid into the body *per anum*, and again, a subsequent treatment with natron. Diodorus' account is probably based on the work of Herodotus, and it is not as detailed (for example, he mentions three grades of funeral but only describes the most expensive which involves evisceration of the body), but he provides some information which is not included by Herodotus.

Despite the shortcomings of the Classical accounts, they enable us to understand the mummification procedure, and modern experiments carried out to assess their accuracy have produced encouraging results. Simulation of the techniques described by Herodotus, to determine their level of accuracy, has been attempted by a number of researchers, including Lucas, Iskander and, in the Manchester project, Garner (David, 1979). His experiments on a series of dead rats indicated that the most expensive method of mummification described by Herodotus did in fact produce the best results in terms of bodily stability and appearance. It was found that a period of thirty or forty days was the maximum required to produce a stable condition in an animal treated with dry natron. This may indeed indicate that, in antiquity, the natron treatment lasted no longer than forty days and the remainder of the seventy-day period that Herodotus specifies for mummification was used for anointing the body and for all the associated religious rites.

The Manchester experiments also indicated the general factors that probably had an impact on the final condition of the body after mummification. These included the use of too little natron, or frequent use of the same natron which would reduce its effectiveness as a dehydrating agent. Natron is a mixture of sodium carbonate and sodium bicarbonate which is found in natural deposits in Egypt; it often contains impurities such as sodium chloride (salt) and sodium sulphate, and variations in the composition of the natron, such as the percentage of impurities, would have caused some variation in its effective use. The stage of decomposition of the body when it first arrived at the embalmer's workshop would have influenced the final result. Finally in the later periods, there was a decline in the embalmers' professional standards as the religious motives for mummification became obscured and the practice became available to many more people (although it was never universal).

The literary accounts are contemporary with the later years of Egyptian civilization, whereas most of the available human remains date to the New Kingdom (*c*.1450 BC). Nevertheless, it is possible to combine both sources to gain some idea of the stages in the mummification procedure.

At death, the family took the corpse to the embalmer's workshop which was called the Pure Place. This was probably a temporary structure such as a tent, which, for important burials, would have been set up next to the tomb; however, for most people, mummification would have been carried out in a communal Pure Place situated somewhere in the necropolis.

The embalmers were a special hereditary class in Egypt who had status and wealth. Their clients could choose from the three methods available according to Herodotus, but relatively few could have afforded the most expensive process which included not only the most extensive preservation of the body but also the most elaborate funerary rites, which would have been performed by the embalmers and their assistants. Wearing masks, they impersonated the gods who were believed to have been present at the embalming of Osiris, the god of death and resurrection, and at least one priest would have presided over the various stages of mummification and, at the completion of each rite, recited the special incantations which are referred to in the Egyptian texts.

The body was stripped and placed on a board, and the process began. The brain was excerebrated (from perhaps as early as the Middle Kingdom, *c.*1900 BC): usually, an iron hook was introduced into the cranial cavity through a passage made into the left nostril and the ethmoid bone (a bone at the base of the skull which forms part of the upper bony nose); the brain was reduced to fragments to facilitate its removal by means of a kind of spatula. The cranial cavity was then probably sluiced out with a fluid to liquefy any remaining tissue. Brain removal was often incomplete, and modern studies provide evidence that some tissue was usually left behind. Since the Egyptians attached no special significance to the function of the brain (they regarded the heart as the seat of the intellect and the emotions), they did not preserve the extracted brain tissue. The cranial cavity was sometimes left empty, or it was filled with resin or resin-soaked linen later in the mummification procedure. Other, less popular, methods of excerebration included intervention through the base of the skull or through a trepanned orbit (Leek, 1969).

The mouth was washed out and packed with resin-soaked linen, and a resinous paste was applied to the face; the eyes were not removed (although few examples have survived, the Leeds Mummy, Natsef-Amun, being a rare and interesting exception), but were allowed to collapse into the orbits. Linen pads were then inserted over the eyeballs and underneath the eyelids, to provide the mummy with false eyes for use in the next life. Greater realism was sought in the 21st and 22nd Dynasties, with the insertion over the eyeballs of artificial eyes made of obsidian and other materials (Lucas, 1934).

The next stage involved the removal of the organs (or viscera) through an abdominal incision in the flank. Diodorus claimed that this was the left flank, and the evidence from most of the mummies confirms this, although there are exceptions to this rule. In some mummies evisceration was not performed, whereas in others there is no abdominal incision and the viscera were removed *per anum*. Nevertheless, it was usual for the embalmer to put his hand into the abdominal cavity through a left-flank incision, and then to cut free and remove the viscera. For this operation, he used a special implement described as a 'sharp Ethiopian knife'. Then, making an additional incision in the diaphragm, he inserted his arm through this and the flank incision to reach the chest cavity and remove the thoracic organs. Religious beliefs prompted the Egyptians to leave the heart *in situ*, since this was regarded as the essential physical part of the person which should not be separated from the body. However, evisceration was frequently imperfect, and sometimes part of or even the whole heart was removed in the process. Diodorus also relates that the kidneys were left in place, but there is no known religious explanation for this, and the modern investigation of mummies has not tended to support this claim. In the 1828 autopsy of the Leeds Mummy, it was stated that the viscera packages contained the kidneys, but unfortunately these are no longer available for study. If kidneys were left *in situ* in the mummies, the most likely explanation is that the embalmers either did not recognize and identify them, or that they were physically more difficult to remove.

According to Diodorus, the body cavities were then washed out with palm wine mixed with various unspecified spices; they were filled with myrrh, cassia and other aromatic substances and, according to Herodotus, this was completed before the treatment with natron. Such a sequence has been disputed, but one feasible suggestion (Lucas, 1962) is that the body was filled with a temporary packing at this stage, probably consisting of dry natron, packets containing a natron and resin mixture, and linen impregnated with resin. This would have assisted the dehydration process, lessened the odour of putrefaction, and would have prevented the collapse of the body wall during further treatment. After the natron treatment was completed, this temporary filling would have been replaced with the permanent stuffing, although here again there were exceptions, and in some mummies there was no packing inside the thoracic and abdominal cavities.

The viscera were also washed with palm wine, mixed with various spices, and then treated with natron as the dehydrating agent. They were subsequently made into four parcels, and these were placed under the protection of the demi-gods known as the Four Sons of Horus. The parcels were dealt with in various ways at different times in Egypt's history: from the 4th Dynasty (*c.*2600 BC) onwards, they were placed inside containers known as canopic jars and kept in the tomb, sometimes inside a special chest. There were four jars to a set, and in some cases the jar-stoppers were represented as human heads, but in others they took the form of the Four Sons, so that Hapy, who protected the lungs, was shown as a baboon, Amset who guarded the liver was human-headed, Duamutef with responsibility for the stomach was represented as jackal-headed, and Qebehsenuef, guardian of the intestines, appeared as a falcon. However, a new custom emerged in the 21st and 22nd Dynasties, when the viscera were made into four parcels, each of which was decorated with a wax image of the appropriate deity, and these were then replaced in the abdominal and thoracic cavities. By the 26th Dynasty (*c.*600 BC), canopic jars were again in use, but in the later years it became a widespread custom to wrap the viscera in one large parcel which was impregnated with spices and placed on the legs of the mummy.

Once the viscera were dealt with, the next important stage was the dehydration of the body itself. Modern methods of preventing decay include the injection of preserving fluids into the blood vessels, deep freezing or freeze-drying. Other ancient societies used the heat of the sun or of fire to desiccate their bodies, and with regard to Egypt, there has been much discussion about the dehydrating agent: did they use salt, lime or natron? (Lucas, 1914; 1932) It is now generally accepted that natron was employed for this purpose, and it also had a range of other uses, including laundering clothes and cleansing the mouth and teeth. There has also been modern controversy over whether natron was employed in a solid state or in the form of a solution when dehydrating the body tissues. This originally arose because of an ambiguity over one of the words in Herodotus' text: an early translation led scholars to conclude that the bodies were immersed and soaked in baths of natron, but re-examination of the Greek and recent experiments on mummified tissue have confirmed that natron, in its natural dry state, was used to pack the bodies, and that this method achieved the most satisfactory results (Sandison, 1963).

The process of dehydration probably took up to forty days, and then the body was lifted from the natron bed, and the natron and temporary stuffing were removed. The body was washed with water to remove all traces of natron and other debris and, since it was still quite pliable, it was now straightened out into the horizontal position. It was at this stage that the embalmers of the 21st Dynasty inserted the packing material under the skin.

It is known that several stages now followed before the body was wrapped in gum-coated strips of linen, but the details of these are uncertain; however, they probably included two distinct processes of anointing the body, using precious oils and fats and odiferous gum-resins. Diodorus claims that the body was first anointed with 'cedar oil' (probably in this case an ordinary oil scented with essential oil of juniper derived from juniper berries) and 'precious ointments' (the ingredients of which are unknown), before it was rubbed with fragrant substances, including myrrh and cinnamon. New stuffing was inserted into the body cavities and the flank incision was closed. In many cases this was not sewn, but the edges of the wound were drawn together and then covered with a metal or beeswax plate which became embedded in the resinous coating which was now applied to the body. The cranial cavity was also packed with strips of linen impregnated with resin, and resin in a molten form may also have been poured into the skull. Resin or wax were used to plug the nostrils, and a further coating of resinous paste was applied to the body. Finally, the body was carefully wrapped in layers of linen bandages, between which the embalmers inserted the amulets, designed to bring magical protection to the deceased; the arms were arranged in their final position, placed either across the chest, or extended alongside the body, varying, to some extent, according to the person's sex or the date of the mummy.

A second anointment then seems to have been performed, and in a special ceremony, the mummy, its coffin, and the viscera (if they were stored in a separate container) were covered with a liquid or semi-liquid resinous substance. Then, the mummy and the funerary goods were taken to the family who could now arrange the burial ceremony in which the mummy and the possessions would be placed in the tomb.

Although the Classical sources refer to the use of resin in mummification, the extent of its employment remains uncertain, as well as its exact nature and source. The Egyptians may have used both gum resins and true resins in mummification, since they had access to both these commodities (Lucas, 1962). Again, it is not evident if bitumen (pitch) played a part in the process; Diodorus and Strabo both claim that the Egyptians imported bitumen (it probably came from the Dead Sea region) and used it for preserving dead bodies, but modern studies have proved inconclusive on this.

Historical Developments in Mummification

Throughout the long history of mummification in ancient Egypt, it is possible to identify a number of significant changes in the techniques that were used.

During the Old Kingdom (*c.*2686–2181 BC), the basic principles were established and employed at first for the royal family and then increasingly for the nobility (who, at this time, were often relatives of the king). Perhaps as early as the 3rd Dynasty (*c.*2650 BC) they abandoned the custom of burying the dead in the foetal position, and henceforth they were arranged so that the body was extended and lying on its left side. Much later (from the New Kingdom onwards), this custom was replaced by laying out the body in the dorsal position.

During the Middle Kingdom (1991–1786 BC), important changes occurred as the result of religious developments at this time. With the collapse of the Old Kingdom and the troubles of the First Intermediate Period, a new political and social order was required, and the Middle Kingdom witnessed many important innovations. In the Old Kingdom, the afterlife had been the exclusive prerogative of the king, and he alone had guaranteed access to immortality. Now, however, the non-royal person became significant and began to expect an individual eternity. The cult of the god Osiris flourished: as king of the underworld who had himself been resurrected from the dead, Osiris was uniquely placed to offer eternal life to his followers, regardless of their wealth or rank. Provided the worshipper had lived a worthy life, Osiris could give him the hope of blessed immortality, even if he had been a person of humble status in this world.

These new ideas brought about profound changes in the funerary customs. Gradually, the nobles and all those who could afford the considerable expenditure adopted the funerary practices once reserved for the royal family. The king's bounty was no longer essential: they now built fine tombs for themselves and equipped them with funerary goods; some of these introduced new forms and ideas, while others were developed from concepts which had been used only for the king and his family. The Pyramid Texts, originally spells to ensure the king's survival after death, were adapted for non-royal persons and inscribed on their coffins (today, we refer to these as Coffin Texts), and the tombs were filled with equipment that included canopic jars, ushabti figures (small models of agricultural workers) and models of brewers, bakers and estate workers. All this was intended to ensure the eternal life of the individual, and to provide within the tomb all the possessions that could bring the owner safety and comfort in his next life. However, even if the deceased did not have the wealth to provide for such a hereafter, he could still hope for immortality, tilling the fields in the kingdom of Osiris.

One result of these beliefs was that new sections of society adopted mummification, although most people continued to be buried in desert graves. However, although more mummies are preserved from this period than from the Old Kingdom, they were not so well prepared and, in most cases, the outcome was less satisfactory. A number of excavators discovered important groups of mummies which date to the Middle Kingdom, such as Maspero, excavating at Thebes in 1883, and de Morgan at Dahshur. In 1903, Naville found the tombs of the princesses while he was excavating the 11th Dynasty mortuary temple of Nebhepetre Mentuhotep at Deir el Bahri, and these mummies were examined by Derry. They showed no evidence of a flank incision to facilitate the removal of the viscera, but there was a tentative suggestion of partial evisceration *per anum*. Some ten years later, the mummies of several other princesses were found in the same area by an American expedition, and in these,

Fig. 6 *A painted panel portrait originally placed over the face of a mummy. Such portraits date to the Ptolemaic period (c. 200 BC), when many Greeks had settled in Egypt. In earlier Pharaonic times mummy masks were stylized and mass-produced, but these later examples were individual likenesses of the owners*

a resinous substance seems to have been injected into the alimentary canal *per annum*. These provide important evidence of how mummification was carried out for the royal family at this period, and they indicate that the bodies of persons of even the highest level were not eviscerated or properly desiccated.

However, some mummies of lesser individuals were eviscerated in the Middle Kingdom, and it was obviously a time of experimentation. It has been mentioned that excerebration was probably introduced, but that less attention was generally given to the actual preservation of the body tissues. Decomposition soon occurred because only a thin coat of resin was applied to the surface of the skin, and this left the desiccation process incomplete. So, although the outward appearance of these mummies, with their fine wrappings, was elaborate, the bandages often concealed skeletal remains and poorly preserved soft tissue, recalling the practices of the Archaic Period.

The troubled Second Intermediate Period (1786–1567 BC) has produced little evidence of its mummification techniques, but in the subsequent New Kingdom (1567–1085 BC) there is an abundant source of information provided by the two caches of mummies discovered in the late nineteenth century (see Chapter 4). Although these royal mummies give information about only one section of the society, it has been possible to identify many of these individuals and to arrange them in a chronological order, so that the techniques used for non-royal mummies can be compared with them and these mummies dated accordingly. Various features have been noted in the royal mummies, which include examples from the 18th through to the 20th Dynasties. Exceptions occur, but generally the positioning of the hands varied according to the sex and date of the individual mummy: in females, the hands were usually placed alongside their thighs, but in males, the arms were fully extended with the hands turned inwards at the side of the thighs. However, in the case of Tuthmosis II (*c*.1512–1504 BC), the arms were crossed over the chest, and this posture was then widely adopted until the 21st Dynasty when the arms were once again extended. In the mummy of Tuthmosis III (1504–1450 BC), the evisceration incision was placed lower in the flank of the mummy and this practice was again continued until the 20th Dynasty (*c*.1160 BC).

By the 19th Dynasty(*c*.1250 BC), various improvements had been introduced. The head of the mummy of King Sethos I is perhaps the finest surviving example of the royal embalmer's skill, and remains in an excellent state of preservation. However, the mummy of his son, Ramesses II, shows an advance in techniques which enabled the embalmers to retain the natural skin colouring, and Ramesses' fair skin is evident (he

Fig. 7 *Another painted panel portrait from the Ptolemaic period, found at Hawara. These were probably painted in the owner's lifetime, perhaps by itinerant artists, and placed in the house. When the owner died, they would be trimmed to shape and incorporated in the mummy wrappings*

Fig. 8 *Gilded cartonnage mask from a mummy, Ptolemaic period. In the later periods, the mummy was no longer buried with treasure as this had so frequently been stolen in the past. Instead, the gold mask and fine jewellery were simulated with a gilded cartonnage mask made of papyrus and gum, set with glass 'stones'*

was a natural redhead). This is in marked contrast to the blackened and discoloured skin of earlier mummies, even that of Sethos I.

Gradually, during the late 19th and early 20th Dynasties, further experimentation brought about the advances which are a feature of the 21st Dynasty, when mummification reached its zenith. The royal mummies of the New Kingdom had suffered great damage as the result of robbers entering the tombs and desecrating the bodies, and, in order to ensure the kings' chances of attaining eternity and continuing to receive sustenance through the offerings in the tomb, the skilled embalmers of the 21st Dynasty tried to partially restore the mummies before reburial. Once they had close contact with the mummies, the embalmers may have become aware of their predecessors' failure to preserve the lifelike appearance and individuality of the deceased rulers, and new measures were introduced to rectify this.

Two methods were available to the embalmers: they could apply padding materials externally to the body to reproduce its contours, a method that had been used with limited success in the Old Kingdom; or they could insert stuffing under the skin surface. This had been attempted towards the end of the 18th Dynasty with the mummy of Amenophis III (1417–1379 BC); because he had been obese in life, it was necessary to simulate his plumpness after death, and so packing was introduced under the skin of the legs, neck and arms. This was the method that the 21st Dynasty embalmers now sought to develop on a wider scale.

A number of royal and priests' mummies of the 21st Dynasty had been discovered in various locations and these were examined in detail by Sir Grafton Elliot Smith who, from his observations, was able to determine the distinctive features of the new method. The viscera were removed through the flank incision and were then packed into four separate parcels, each containing the appropriate guardian from the Four Sons of Horus. However, the parcels were no longer stored in canopic jars but were returned, with other packing material, to the body cavities. The heart was still left in place, and the embalmers continued to remove the brain. However, they now attempted to recreate the bodily contours: in addition to the viscera parcels, the body cavity was packed through the flank incision with materials such as sawdust, butter, linen and mud, and the incision was plugged with linen; to simulate the body shape, packing was also introduced under the skin through a series of small surface incisions. Neck and facial packing was also used, the latter being inserted through the mouth.

Other details were added so that the mummy could be more readily identified with its owner. Artificial eyes, made of limestone, calcite or bone, or of balls of linen with the pupils delineated in black paint were fixed in the orbits; the face and sometimes the whole body were painted with red ochre (for men) and yellow ochre (for women); and false plaits and curls were added to augment the owner's natural hair. The positioning of the hands varied: in the male and female royal mummies, the hands were placed alongside their hips, while in the case of the priests, the hands were extended over the genital organs. The mummy of Nodjme, the wife of Herihor (who, as High Priest of Amun, wielded unprecedented and almost royal power), is an interesting example of the transition from the old to new techniques at the beginning of the 21st Dynasty (*c.*1095

BC). Here, as in earlier times, the body is built up by means of external padding, but also (although there is no attempt to introduce subcutaneous packing) the embalmers have introduced such innovations as facial stuffing (sawdust) through the mouth and artificial eyes.

In the later periods, the standards of mummification declined, although the new techniques were retained in the 22nd and 23rd Dynasties (*c*.945–715 BC). After this, more attention was paid to the external appearance of the mummy and its wrappings than to the preservation of the body. By the 26th Dynasty (*c*.600 BC), subcutaneous packing had almost entirely ceased, and the viscera, wrapped in parcels, were now usually either placed between the legs or stored in the canopic jars that had been reintroduced as part of the funerary furniture.

The conquest of Egypt by the Greeks and subsequently by the Romans brought about the final developments in mummification. The foreigners who now settled in Egypt often adopted the native funerary beliefs and customs, probably finding them a comforting alternative to their own rather nebulous concepts of the hereafter. Consequently, mummification was adopted by many more people, but increasingly in the Ptolemaic Period (332–30 BC) it became a social and commercial rather than religious concern.

In general, the mummies were now poorly preserved; in some instances, the viscera were removed and treated but then returned to the body cavities in a random order, whereas in others, the body was either packed with balls of resin-soaked linen, mud or broken pottery, or filled with molten resin or possibly bitumen. Mud and linen were also inserted into the mouth and the orbits. Sometimes evisceration was not performed at all and there was often no attempt to remove the brain. Extensive use was made of resin as an embalming agent, with the result that the skin is blackened and is frequently hard and shiny. Not only was molten resin applied directly to the skin surface, but it was also poured into the body cavity through the flank incision and into the skull through the nostril or foramen magnum, in the cases where the brain had been removed. Maggots and beetles (which were already using the decomposing body as a food source) were often trapped and killed between the bandage layers by the molten resin, and these have been found by modern investigators. They show that many bodies were in an advanced state of decomposition before the process of mummification was started. Radiological studies have provided further evidence of this: sometimes, the contents of the wrappings are in complete confusion and even incorporate the bones of more than one individual, while in other cases the head has become detached from the body or limbs are found to

Fig. 9 *Gilded cartonnage covering the mummy of a child, dating from the Roman period (1st century AD). As the technique of mummification declined, more attention was paid to the elaborate outer wrapping of the body; however, x-rays often show that the mummy inside was poorly preserved*

be missing. The general conclusion is that the bodies had fallen apart during mummifcation.

Various explanations have been offered for this. Since there was now a marked increase in the numbers of those seeking mummification, there would have been a decline in standards and also a delay in starting work on the cheaper burials. However, Herodotus offers another explanation, relating that the bodies of certain women (those who had been beautiful or the wives of eminent men) were only handed over to the embalmers some three or four days after death, when decomposition would have commenced. This was intended to inhibit or prevent necrophilia in the embalmer's workshop.

The mummies of the Ptolemaic Period that survive today in museums give no outward hint that they are poor examples of the embalmer's craft. Fine linen bandages are often exquisitely pleated in geometric patterns, decorated with interspersed gilt studs, and the mummy is adorned with brightly painted cartonnage. Cartonnage (literally, an outer covering) was made from waste paper (which sometimes included fragments of papyrus documents) and gum, and was used to fashion the three units now attached to the mummy. One piece enclosed the head and shoulders and was painted to represent a stylized face and headdress; another decorated with representations of amulets, jewellery, and religious rites, covered the chest; and the third, on which a pair of sandals was shown, was placed over the feet. During this period, another innovation was to place over the face of the mummy a portrait of the deceased, painted (probably during the owner's lifetime) on a wooden panel.

After the Romans established their rule in Egypt (30 BC), mummification suffered a period of further decline. The bodies are usually poorly preserved and it is often not possible to establish if brain removal and evisceration were carried out; the custom was simply to apply a thick resinous coating to the surface of the body. However, this lowering of standards is not evident in the outward appearance of the mummy, for many are enclosed in bandages decorated with painted religious scenes and gilded head and chest covers, often moulded and inlaid with coloured glass to represent the jewellery which they no longer took with them into the tomb.

As this period unfolded and the country was converted to Christianity, mummification was still practised in parts of Egypt and Nubia. With new religious beliefs, it was no longer required that the individual physical likeness should be retained in the mummy, and evisceration was also discontinued, but they still attempted to preserve the body. The skin surface was spread with natron and other substances, to make the skin soft and pliable, and, in place of the layers of bandages, the body was dressed in embroidered clothes and boots and wrapped in linen sheets. With the Arab invasion of Egypt in AD 641 and the introduction and subsequent spread of Islam, mummification finally ceased and the old funerary customs came to an end.

4 The Discovery and 1828 Autopsy of Natsef-Amun

A.R. David

The region known today as Deir el Bahri lies on the west bank of the Nile opposite the modern town of Luxor where Thebes once stood; in antiquity, it formed part of the great necropolis where the inhabitants of Thebes were buried. Today, Deir el Bahri is dominated by the magnificent mortuary temple of the 18th Dynasty ruler, Queen Hatshepsut (1503–1482 BC); tiered and terraced, this was designed to stand against the backdrop of the Theban cliffs, but it probably drew much of its inspiration and certainly its building stone from the neighbouring 11th Dynasty pyramid and temple complex which belonged to Nebhepetre Mentuhotep and of which only the foundations now survive.

Many archaeological expeditions came to work at Thebes from the time of Napoleon. Such excavations were not always accurately recorded, particularly in the early years, so that the exact location of some of the tombs and details of the objects found in them have not survived. However, at Deir el Bahri, in addition to the two temples, a number of important cemeteries were uncovered and recorded and it was also the site where important caches of mummies were discovered.

The royal tombs in the Valley of the Kings (a short distance away over the mountain from Deir el Bahri) had, with the exception of Tutankhamun's tomb, been extensively plundered in antiquity. Later rulers attempted to stop the plundering of the dead pharaohs and nobles, and to rescue them by collecting the

Fig. 10 *The temple of Queen Hatshepsut at Deir el Bahri. This magnificent funerary temple was built during the 18th Dynasty for the worship of the deified queen after her death. The area later became a centre for the burial of numbers of priests and priestesses, and it was probably near here that Passalacqua found the mummy and coffins of Natsef-Amun*

surviving mummies and reburying them in a communal tomb where they hoped that the remains might be more secure. By the 21st Dynasty the nobles were no longer building individual tombs, but instead used small intrusive burials in older tombs, or hid large caches of coffins and bodies in remote places in the Theban cliffs. The rulers of this dynasty decided to conceal the royal mummies in the same way, by burying them in secret hiding-places, and by the order of the High Priest of Amun, Herihor, the bodies of Ramesses II and of his father, Sethos I, were restored and rewrapped. Later, in the Valley of the Kings, the mummies of Ramesses I and II were moved from their own tombs to that of Sethos I, and on two subsequent occasions these three bodies were transferred to other burial places. However, it was decided that the Deir el Bahri area would be more secure, and King Psusennes III ordered these bodies, together with many other royal mummies of the New Kingdom and of his own family, to be transferred to a new site – a shaft in a little valley to the south of the temple area at Deir el Bahri. Probably, at the same time, another group of nine royal mummies were reburied in the tomb of Amenophis II.

The Deir el Bahri cache remained hidden until, in AD 1872, the local fellahin discovered the burial place, subsequently plundering the site and removing many of the smaller antiquities that they found with the mummies. They sold these to foreign tourists and collectors, and thus objects belonging to the

Theban priest-rulers of the 21st Dynasty came on to the market, alerting scholars that a royal tomb of some sort had been found and was being systematically plundered. However, it was not until 1881 that the authorities, under the Director of Antiquities, Gaston Maspero, were able to gain from the locals the secret of the whereabouts of this tomb and to trace it. When they found it, the tomb was cleared and the royal mummies were secured for the Cairo Museum, where Grafton Elliot Smith subsequently made a detailed study of them (Smith, 1912; also Maspero, 1889 and Daressy, 1909).

This great Deir el Bahri cache was found to contain the mummies not only of some members of the ruling family of the 21st Dynasty priests of Amun, but also of some of the most famous kings of the New Kingdom, together with their queens and family members, ranging from the 17th to the 20th Dynasties. However, the series of these rulers was incomplete and Maspero searched further, suspecting that a second collection remained to be found. It was Loret, another French Egyptologist, who discovered the tomb of Amenophis II in 1898 when he was working in the Valley of the Kings, and this contained not only the king's mummy but also some of those missing from the Deir el Bahri sequence, as well as those of several queens and princesses.

Other discoveries were made at Deir el Bahri when, in 1858 and 1891, in the area of Hatshepsut's temple, two great caches of mummies were found which had belonged to the priests of Montu and of Amun. Georges Daressy, a French Egyptologist, carried out excavations here under both Maspero and Grébaut. In January 1891, when the Antiquities Service was clearing sand from the upper terrace of the temple, pits were discovered in front of the temple, covered with sand and stones. Daressy was brought in to undertake the excavation of this area, and he recounts (Daressy, 1900) how, on entering the galleries of a re-used family tomb, he realized that he had discovered a small cache, similar to the great cache found by Maspero ten years earlier. However, the style of the coffins now indicated that this burial dated to the end of the 21st Dynasty and included not kings and high priests but lower ranking priests and priestesses attached to the cult of Amun.

The coffins in the tomb had been placed in both galleries, but they were in some disarray; presumably their owners had not prepared individual tombs and, perhaps to increase their chance of cheating the tomb robbers, they had chosen to be buried communally. This cache contained one hundred and fifty-three coffins, as well as a collection of statues, stelae, canopic jars, sandals, garlands, funerary offerings, and other goods. It took nine days to clear the tomb, and the objects were taken to Cairo by river, where they were studied and put on public display in 1892. Most items remained there, although some of the coffins, stelae and other goods were eventually dispersed to museums and collections around the world. A general paucity of material from the 21st Dynasty (partly due to the removal of the capital from Thebes to Tanis in the Delta, where environmental conditions are less favourable for the preservation of ancient sites) is offset, to some extent, by the information about individual names and titles which is inscribed on the coffins found in these caches (Daressy, 1896 and 1907); and the examination of mummies found in this context has provided useful information about the development of contemporary funerary practices (Daressy and Smith, 1903).

On 2 February 1828, William Osburn read a communication to the Leeds Literary and Philosophical Society, of which he was secretary. This gave a short account of the mummy of a priest, Natsef-Amun, and said: 'Not more than six months after its arrival at Leeds, I stated my conviction that the individual had been an inhabitant of Thebes in Upper Egypt and that the Mummy was from the Catacombs of Gournor, the burial place of that city.' Subsequent information enabled Osburn to say with some certainty that this mummy had been discovered in Egypt by the Italian Giuseppe (Joseph) Passalacqua and sent to Trieste in 1823. Then, through a series of purchases, the mummy had finally come into the possession of the museum owned by the Leeds Society.

Passalacqua (1797–1865), an Italian, was born at Trieste. Like Giovanni Belzoni, he had originally travelled to Egypt on a different business enterprise (horse-dealing, in this case) which had not prospered. Consequently, he turned his hand to excavation and collecting antiquities. He managed to put together a large and important collection of antiquities drawn from Thebes and other Egyptian sites, which was described in his *Catalogue* (Passalacqua, 1826). In 1822–5, Passalacqua was working at Thebes, and it was probably during his excavation of the tombs of priests and priestesses of Amun in the causeway area of Hatshepsut's temple at Deir el Bahri that the mummy and coffins of Natsef-Amun were found (Porter and Moss, 1989). With the hope of selling his collection, he brought it to Paris in 1826 and exhibited it at 52, Passage Vivienne. The collection was offered to the French government for the sum of 400,000 francs, but they rejected it, and most of the objects were eventually taken to Berlin, where Frederich Wilhelm IV of Prussia bought them for the museum collection. He paid only 100,000 francs for the antiquities, but Passalacqua accompanied them and became, until his death in 1865, the conservator of Egyptian collections in the Berlin Museum.

Osburn's assumptions about the find-spot of Natsef-Amun's mummy and coffins were, as he says in his communication, borne out by comments that he read in a personal narrative by Passalacqua which accompanied a catalogue of a museum of Egyptian antiquities in Paris. Dating to 1823, this stated that Passalacqua had sent 'two remarkably fine mummies from Gournor to Trieste', and that, when he later returned to Trieste, he understood that they had been 'transmitted to London'. From this and other circumstantial information, Osburn was able to infer that one of these 'Passalacqua mummies' was indeed that of the priest Natsef-Amun.

The Leeds Society had acquired this mummy to enable the members to expand their scientific studies on mummified remains (see Chapter 6). It was autopsied in 1828, and in Chapter 11 an account is given of the medical evidence derived from that investigation, comparing it with the current study. This autopsy was one of the earliest scientific examinations to be undertaken on an Egyptian mummy: a multidisciplinary approach was adopted, involving specialists in several fields, and the results were promptly published (Osburn, 1828). In this account, Osburn describes how the mummy was unwrapped and autopsied, and gives details of various features of the mummy, its wrappings and the associated artefacts; in the appendices there is an account by E. S. George of the chemical examination of some of the substances connected with the mummy, and T. P. Teale describes his anatomical study of certain parts of the mummy, which were placed in the society's museum in Leeds. The publication also includes a discussion of the symbolism of the mythological paintings found on the coffins, and an attempted translation of the hieroglyphic inscriptions that accompanied the mummy.

This account was produced at the request of the council of the Leeds Society, to provide an explanation of the study of the mummy, and because 'so many new, and in their opinion, important facts presented themselves during the process of unwrapping the body, that the Council conceived they would have been wanting in the interests of the Society had they forborne to make them public.'

There is a discussion in the account about the name and titles of the priest: Osburn read his name as Natsef-Amun (Osburn, 1828) and although the correct version is now known to be Esamun (Porter and Moss, 1989), the earlier version has been retained in the current study because it has been in general use for so long in Leeds.

The mummy was originally enclosed in two coffins, one fitting inside the other; a bituminous substance had been poured over the mummy at the time of embalming, and in 1828 patches of this substance still remained, causing the mummy to adhere to the bottom of the inner coffin. Both coffins are anthropoid and mummiform; the inner one represents the deceased wrapped in a white garment decorated with two yellow vertical borders of hieroglyphic inscriptions, while, on the head, there is a representation of a headband with a lotus in the centre of the front. Over the chest, a winged scarab (symbolizing resurrection) is depicted, and there is a painted bead and floral collar, below which another scene shows a sacred barque holding the scarab beetle and the kneeling goddesses, Isis and Nephthys. Another goddess, also kneeling, is depicted lower down on the coffin.

The outer coffin consists of a top and a base, and was constructed from several pieces of sycamore fastened together with wooden pins. Osburn observes that 'The carpentry appears to have been rude; but all the interstices are filled up with plaster, a thick coat of which also covers the whole surface, both external and internal' (Osburn, 1828). The coffin is a fine example of the craftsmanship of this period, and is decorated with the traditional range of mythological scenes, painted on to a deep yellow background.

The top half of the coffin lid represents a stylized but well-executed face. Such funerary goods were mass-produced and bought from stock, and would have borne no resemblance to the owner. The wooden beard has been broken off, but the large head-dress is clearly represented, carved and painted as an elaborate wig with quantities of hair woven into small braids which hang down over the shoulders. Around the wig, a wreath of Persea is painted, with a lotus flower and two leaves suspended over the crown of the head to hang down over the forehead. A great bead collar, which includes a winged scarab in its centre, is painted around the neck, and the arms are represented as crossed over the chest, although the crook and flail once held in the hands are now missing. Across the body of the coffin, below the arms, the sacred barque is depicted and below this, the figure of the sky goddess is shown kneeling with her wings outstretched.

The lower part of the coffin is decorated with three vertical lines of inscription that run down the centre; on either side of these there are four scenes showing the deceased making offerings and addressing various deities. These scenes are separated from each other by horizontal lines of hieroglyphs. The base of the coffin at head level is painted with a scene that shows the winged figure of the goddess Isis, kneeling on the hieroglyphic sign for gold; she is flanked by the Four Sons of Horus. The two sides of the coffin base are each divided into nine compartments, each of which contains one or more gods in addition to a hieroglyphic inscription. On the right-hand side

Fig. 11 *The outer coffin of Natsef-Amun. This is a particularly fine coffin, decorated with scenes of deities who would protect the owner in the afterlife. The face is stylized and makes no attempt to represent the features of the priest*

*The outer coffin of
Natsef-Amun.*
Fig. 12 (above) *Side-view*

Fig. 13 (below left)
Head end

Fig. 14 (below right)
Foot end

(from the head end), the compartment scenes depict various deities: Ptah-Soker (accompanied by Hathor) holds various sceptres and stands before an altar piled high with fruit and flowers; Thoth, holding a standard surmounted by the symbols of a star and the sky, stands before the seated figure of Osiris, who is accompanied by Isis; the rest of the gods, shown as mummiform figures, each standing before an offering table, are Geb, Nut, Horus, Thoth, Selkis, Serket and Nephthys.

On the left-hand side of the coffin base (again from the head

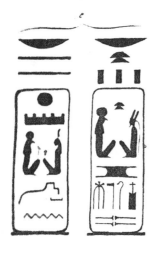

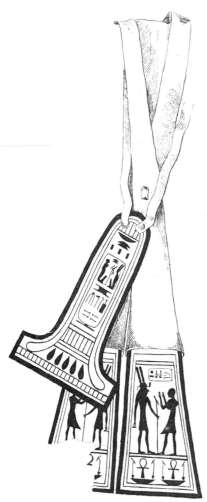

end), the compartment scenes depict Ptah-Soker (followed by Hathor) who holds sceptres and stands before an altar; Thoth, standing with one arm outstretched in front of an altar, and facing Re-Harakhte, who is accompanied by Ma'at; and the other gods, mummiform figures who each stand before an offering table and include Amun, Khepri, Shu, Tefnut, Nefertem, Bennu and Anubis. Under the foot of the coffin there are two scenes: the lid scene shows Nephthys kneeling on the gold sign and holding two *ankh* signs (to give life) in her outstretched arms, while the scene on the base depicts Isis and Nephthys adoring the Djed pillar, the symbol of stability.

As on most mummy cases, the scenes and hieroglyphic inscriptions were intended to provide the deceased with the protection of magic, and a means of successfully meeting the challenges of the Day of Judgement and so reaching the land of Osiris, the god of the underworld. The spells were taken from the Book of Gates, one of the sacred texts which, from the New Kingdom onwards, were used to assist the deceased in his perilous journey into the next world. Similarly, the gods depicted on the coffins were there to give help to the owner and to ensure that he attained immortality.

The mummy of Natsef-Amun was originally wrapped in quantities of linen cloth 'nowhere less than forty thicknesses', but much of this was removed in the 1828 autopsy. At that time, fragments of a very fine white linen which had formed the outermost layer still adhered to the underlying bandages, which were of a coarser quality, each about a foot in width and 'steeped in a dark coloured gum'. They were wound around the body from head to foot in some five or six thicknesses and they secured the wrappings underneath. These were coarser and broader bandages, and it was here, between the folds, that the investigators found a floral necklet which echoed the details of collars represented on many statues and figures shown in tomb and temple wall scenes. It was made of two garlands, one resting on top of the other; the upper one consisted of nine double strings, composed of red berries and lotus flower petals, while the second garland, placed nearer the body, was made up of nine single strings which also included lotus petals. Osburn observed: 'The execution of these intricate pieces of flower-work is very neat and accurate.' He also noted that the garland painted on the coffin recreated in detail this necklet of real flowers.

Further down in the linen folds and placed over the bandages that enclosed the head and face, the unwrapping next revealed the presence of an ornament, composed of several strips of red leather, some of which had broken off, because of the brittle state of the leather, and lay within the bandage layers. This

Fig. 15 *Drawings of the leather ornament or brace found inside the wrappings of Natsef-Amun's mummy. It is decorated with figures of gods, and with a hieroglyphic inscription which includes the names of Ramesses XI in two cartouches (ovals), enabling the mummy to be dated precisely to this king's reign*

brace was decorated with figures of deities and hieroglyphs which Osburn claimed were 'evidently the impressions of heated metal types'. The inscription included the names, in two cartouches, of Ramesses XI (wrongly identified in 1828 as Ramesses V).

Further down, the unwrapping revealed several larger pieces of linen, laid on the body, and these were of the three textures observed in the other bandages. One proved to be a garment, 'a piece of cloth doubled and seamed together on two sides, like a bag'; the neck aperture and the armholes were hemmed, and a fringe decorated the bottom of the garment. Examination of the bandages revealed that there had been re-use of some textiles; there were seams in a number of pieces, and others had been mended. From the evidence provided by this mummy and by others, it seems that the embalmers utilized old garments and other textiles to wrap the body. Medium-quality linen bandages were used to tightly wrap the hands and arms, which were slightly bent at the elbow so that the hands met in front; the hands were amputated at the wrists in the autopsy and have subsequently been kept separately from the body.

Underneath the bandages, every part of the body was covered with a 'thick layer of spicery' which was 'nowhere less than an inch [2.5cm] in thickness'. This mixture also filled the thoracic and abdominal cavities, and Osburn observed that 'in its dry state, it still retains the faint smell of cinnamon or cassia which it has imported to everything in its vicinity: but when mixed with alcohol or water, or exposed to the action of heat, the odour of myrrh becomes very powerfully predominant'. Cassia wood and cinnamon wood are frequently mentioned in translations of Egyptian texts, and both spices (which are the dried bark of certain varieties of laurel that grow in India, Ceylon and China) were known to the Classical writers. However, examples of their use in mummification are not well documented: apart from Osburn's uncertain identification here, Pettigrew refers (Pettigrew, 1834) to a mummy which he examined where the cavity was 'merely filled with the dust of cedar, cassia, etc. and an earthy matter' (Lucas, 1962). The cavity of Natsef-Amun's mouth was also filled with a powdered vegetable substance, and the cavity of the cranium was more than half-filled with spices ground to a coarse powder, amongst which a few lumps of resinous material were found. The chemical analysis of samples taken from the mummy indicated the presence of myrrh and cassia, of gelatine, tannin, resin and natron. The latter occurred in the form of small white crystals on the skin surface and bandages which, when analyzed, were found to consist 'almost entirely of carbonate of soda, with some muriate and sulphate' (natron) (Osburn, 1828; Lucas, 1962). A material resembling wax was also identified (see Chapter 11). Generally, the evidence suggests that the mummy was carefully prepared and that expensive woods and resins were used.

Osburn stated: 'The body is in an unusually perfect state of preservation.' The mummification techniques used for Natsef-Amun indicate that the body dates to the late 20th or early 21st Dynasty, and this corresponds with the inscriptional evidence which places him in the reign of Ramesses XI, the last king of the 20th Dynasty. Under the thick layer of pounded spices, it was observed that the mummy had skin 'of a livid grey colour, soft and greasy to touch'. The facial features were shrivelled, the eyes remained in the orbits, and the tongue protruded through the mouth (possible reasons for this are discussed elsewhere, pp 116–7, 145). As a priest, the head, eyebrows and beard had all been closely shaved, and the short hairs of his beard were reported to 'only appear under the chin'. The viscera had been removed through an incision in the left side of the abdomen and this was not subsequently closed with any type of suture. Osburn claimed that the heart, liver and kidneys had all been removed, treated with natron, made into packages, and returned to the left side of the thoracic cavity. The brain had also been extracted through the right nostril. In general, the mummy had been prepared according to the most elaborate method described in the Classical writers, but there was no evidence of subcutaneous packing, although the facial cavities had been filled with sawdust.

The 1828 unwrapping, autopsy, dissection and examination of this mummy provide an excellent example of an early multidisciplinary study, and the mummy itself illustrates important developments in the technical development of mummification. Further studies, including a radiological survey and a dental examination, were undertaken in 1931 and 1964, and from these various investigations, it was concluded that Natsef-Amun had been middle-aged when he died, that there was some evidence of disease (unspecified) during adolescence, that his estimated height was 5ft 6in and that his well-manicured and hennaed fingernails reflected his privileged lifestyle.

5 Natsef-Amun's Life as a Priest

A.R. David

Natsef-Amun, according to his coffin inscription, was a priest at Karnak who held the title of 'Scribe of Accounts of the Cattle of the Estate of Amun'. He was also an incense-bearer and a Scribe in the Shrine of Montu, the Lord of Thebes; a *wāāb* priest; and a Scribe of the Oblations made to all the gods of Upper and Lower Egypt. Within the bandages that enclosed his mummy, some five or six folds from the surface, the investigators at the 1828 autopsy found a red leather ornament or brace which resembled a bunch of lotus flowers. This, placed across the face of the mummy, was perhaps a badge of office since it bore the name, stamped in hieroglyphs, of King Ramesses XI in whose reign (1113–1085 BC) Natsef-Amun probably lived and worked. To understand the background to this period, it is necessary to consider the earlier part of the New Kingdom.

The 19th Dynasty (1320–1200 BC) was established with the brief reign of Ramesses I, a soldier to whom Horemheb (who was also originally a military man) had handed the throne. His son, Sethos I, and grandson, Ramesses II, rebuilt Egypt's power and prestige abroad after it was allowed to lapse in the reign of the heretic pharaoh, Akhenaten (Amenophis IV). They constructed great temples at Abydos, Thebes and Abu Simbel, and Egypt again enjoyed stability and prosperity. However, their immediate descendants, Merneptah and Ramesses III, had to contend with new dangers from abroad in the form of the Sea-peoples, and the later Ramesside kings (Ramesses IV to XI) ruled over a ‑country which was gradually disintegrating. This was evident in the failing food supplies, strikes and tomb

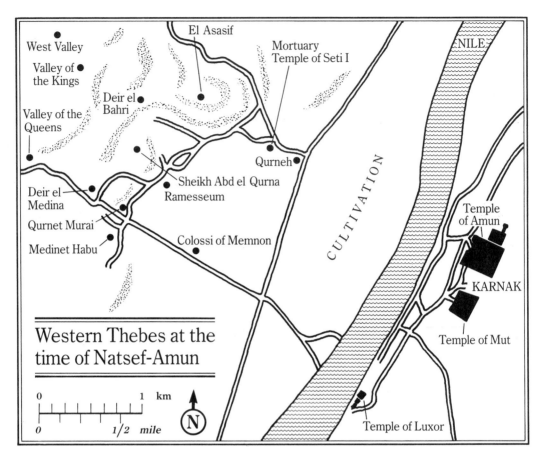

West Valley

Valley of the Kings

Valley of the Queens

Deir el Bahri

El Asasif

Mortuary Temple of Seti I

NILE

Deir el Medina

Qurnet Murai

Medinet Habu

Sheikh Abd el Qurna

Ramesseum

Qurneh

Colossi of Memnon

CULTIVATION

Temple of Amun

KARNAK

Temple of Mut

Temple of Luxor

Western Thebes at the time of Natsef-Amun

0   1   km

0   1/2   mile

N

robberies, and towards the end of Ramesses IX's reign (1140–1121 BC), the royal necropolis workmen who lived near Thebes at the town site known today as Deir el Medina experienced severe problems (Černý, 1973). They were terrorized by foreigners (who were either new arrivals or descendants of earlier prisoners-of-war), and famine in Egypt resulted in the delay of their food rations. The consequent unrest led to a series of strikes amongst the workmen who were engaged in building and decorating the royal tombs, and there was also a spate of tomb robberies in which some of them were implicated. Papyri including the Abbott, Amherst and Mayer A provide a detailed account of the tomb robberies and the state trials which began in Ramesses IX's reign and lasted for many years (Peet, 1930).

In this reign, the weakness of the central government again became apparent, and the danger of a too-powerful priesthood rivalling the king's supremacy re-emerged. By Year 10 of Ramesses IX's reign, the High Priest of Amun at Thebes, a man named Amenhotep, had succeeded in acquiring great personal power by controlling the god's wealth and estates. His position had become hereditary and, in all but name, the high priests of Amun stood equal with the king, who had taken up residence in the north of Egypt. Indeed, Amenhotep underlined his status by having his figure represented the same size as the king in two temple wall scenes.

The next ruler, Ramesses X, had only a brief reign. Under Ramesses XI (1113–1085 BC, who was the last king of the 20th Dynasty (1200–1085 BC), the final cleavage occurred between the kings in the north and the high priests of Amun in the south. At first the king continued to rule the whole country from the north; then perhaps at the royal request, the Viceroy of Nubia, Panehsy, intervened against the High Priest Amenhotep at Thebes, taking the southern district for himself and claiming its resources, as well as the supreme command of the army. Panehsy thus became the effective ruler of Upper and Middle Egypt in addition to Nubia, although he was still nominally under the control of Ramesses XI, but he fell into disgrace, and a new man – Herihor – became High Priest of Amun and Viceroy of Nubia. Originally an army general, he became the first commoner in Egypt to combine the ability to use great military power, to rule over Nubia, and to hold the high-priesthood at Thebes, where he took care to ensure that his accession was endorsed by the gods.

In Year 19 of Ramesses XI's reign, a Renaissance Era was proclaimed; in earlier reigns, the occurrence of such an event (known as the Repeating of Births) was regarded as the commencement of a great new era. A new political arrangement emerged, with Herihor ruling at Thebes, while in the north a man of unknown origin named Smendes was appointed (with status parallel to Herihor) as the king's supreme executive. Nominally, both Smendes and Herihor were still subject to Ramesses XI, so that from this date, Egypt and Nubia were effectively divided into two great provinces, with the boundary fixed at El Hibeh, each controlled by one man who owed superficial allegiance to the king. This political arrangement was to last for some three hundred years.

In the south, Herihor assumed great power. In one area of the Temple of Khonsu at Karnak, wall inscriptions name the king as Ramesses XI while Herihor is merely recorded as high priest of Amun, but in the forecourt Herihor is referred to as king; his name is written in the cartouches (ovals) reserved for the names of pharaohs and he is accorded a royal titulary. His kingship is also proclaimed in inscriptions that occur in the Great Hypostyle Hall in the Temple of Amun at Karnak, as well as on funerary equipment which belonged to his family. On this evidence, Egyptologists of the nineteenth century believed that Herihor had actually supplanted Ramesses XI as king and founded a dynasty of priest kings at Thebes, but the limits of his rulership are now recognized. Since his royal claims are found only at Thebes, the centre of his power, he almost certainly never assumed the overall kingship of the country, but remained subordinate in name at least to Ramesses XI.

In Year 5 of the Renaissance Era, Herihor sent an emissary named Wenamun to Byblos on the Syrian coast, to acquire timber which was needed for a new state barque for the god Amun. The events of this journey are recalled in the literary piece 'The Tale of Wenamun', which provides ample evidence that Egypt's prestige abroad had fallen considerably from the earlier years of the New Kingdom. Egypt's Asiatic provinces, once part of a proud empire, had been lost soon after the death of Ramesses III (1199–1166 BC), and her influence had waned. However, contact with countries to the north was maintained, and Ramesses XI apparently sent a gift of exotic pets – a crocodile and an ape – to the Assyrian king, Assur-bel-kala.

Herihor died before Ramesses XI, and was succeeded in the south by his son Piankh, who was probably the child of his wife Nodjme, whose mummy was found in the great cache at Thebes. Piankh had been the High Steward of Amun and Prophet of Mut and Khonsu (Amun's wife and son) at Karnak; when he inherited his father's position, this established a family dynasty of military high priests of Amun at Thebes. However, the family did not gain overall control of the country; when Ramesses XI died, it was Smendes, the northern chief (and possibly Ramesses XI's son-in-law) who became king of Egypt (1089–1063 BC) and the first ruler of the 21st Dynasty. The virtual division of Egypt continued throughout this dynasty (c.1089–945 BC), with a line of kings nominally ruling in the north from the city of Tanis, while the high priests of Amun controlled the south from Thebes.

The reign of Ramesses XI marked the end of the New Kingdom; he was possibly the last ruler to be buried at Thebes in the Valley of the Kings, and his successors moved the state capital to Tanis in the Delta. During his reign, Nubia, refusing to acknowledge Herihor's overlordship, broke away from Egypt and followed an independent course for many years; in Syria/Palestine, none of Egypt's former possessions remained and her influence in the area had long since been lost.

It was against the background of these troubled times that Natsef-Amun lived and worked as a priest in the Temple of Amun at Karnak, at the very centre of the power struggle between the king and the high priests. Amun was Egypt's most wealthy deity, and Natsef-Amun would have enjoyed many privileges. The Egyptian phrase we translate as priest had the exact meaning of 'god's servant'. These men were functionaries who acted on behalf of the king (who was the god's son) in the temples, caring for the deity's needs through the regular and unceasing performance of rituals, and thus ensuring that the state religion was perpetuated. In this way, it was believed, the equilibrium of the universe would be maintained and continued, the king would gain immortality and success over his enemies, and the fertility of the land and its people would be assured.

However, the priests were never regarded as a special sect who were set apart because they had received a divine revelation, and the temples were the houses of the gods and not places of congregational worship. Indeed, the priests had no pastoral duties, and they were not expected to preach or to convert the masses; the people's personal worship was generally conducted away from the temples, in the privacy of their own homes, and was usually addressed to deities who were far removed from the state gods. Most priests were probably dedicated officials, stately in their deportment and wise in their conduct. The ancient Instructions in Wisdom – the guidelines for those who would occupy high office – emphasize the moral and social requirements as discretion in speech, honesty, and appropriate behaviour towards others. Nevertheless, the priests were essentially functionaries who performed the rituals and their thoughts and actions beyond their temple duties were not of paramount importance. There was no concept of vocation, and the relative wealth and privilege offered by a career in the priesthood probably attracted ambitious and sometimes unscrupulous candidates.

The role of god's servant is one of the oldest in Egypt. In the earliest communities of predynastic Egypt, the village leaders undoubtedly acted as priests, presenting food regularly at the shrine of the local god so that the well-being of the people would

Fig. 16 *The Temple of Amun at Karnak. Amun is usually shown as a human figure, but his sacred animal was the ram, represented at Karnak by the avenues of ram-headed sphinxes. His original consort was Amaunet, but at Karnak and in the nearby Temple of Luxor, the vulture-goddess Mut was his wife*

be ensured. Throughout the historic period, down to the Graeco-Roman era, the essential character of this role remained the same; it offered many advantages and yet entry did not necessarily require the priests to be profound thinkers, to have great theological knowledge, or to be men of spirituality (although some undoubtedly expressed all these qualities).

Recruitment to the priesthood occurred in a number of ways. The most common tradition was for the son to follow his father, as in most trades and professions in ancient Egypt. According to Herodotus, 'When a priest dies, his son is put in his place,' and there are examples of particular priesthoods continuing in the same family for as many as seventeen generations. In the 21st Dynasty, the offices of the major priesthoods of Amun and of the high priest of Ptah at Memphis were all hereditary, and men sought to confirm the right to inherit the priesthood at this time. Nevertheless, this right was always ultimately in the gift of the pharaoh, although he rarely intervened in such appointments. However, he did on occasion promote a priest whose perform- ance of his duties had been notable or praiseworthy in some way, and the royal right was actively exercized in the appoint- ment of the high priests when it was necessary to adjust the balance of power. Then, the king could introduce new blood by selecting a high priest from another priesthood, or from his own Court, or from among his army generals, rather than promoting an internal candidate from the god's own priesthood. Other methods of recruitment included the selection of candidates by a committee of priests, when there were vacancies to be filled, and the approval of such a committee was probably required as a formality even when the candidate inherited the post. On other occasions, an office could be purchased on the payment of a fee – a practice which occurred at least as early as the Middle Kingdom and became most widespread in the Graeco-Roman Period.

After appointment, the novice priest probably served a form of apprenticeship when he learnt the background to the religious ceremonies and practised the rituals needed to serve the god. There may have been an installation, when the priest was presented at the temple and perhaps received a ritual baptism and purification, before being allowed to look upon the god's statue, housed in the temple sanctuary. At some stage, the priest was also probably initiated into the secret knowledge of the god's cult.

An important aspect of the Egyptian temple was that it employed mostly lay priests, who were in the majority in the Old and Middle Kingdoms. Later, when a class of permanent priests was established in the larger temples, lay priests still dominated in the smaller institutions. Each temple had four

Fig. 17 *The Temple of Amun at Karnak. Each Egyptian cultus temple was considered to be the original place of creation – a fertile island with lush vegetation – and this was recreated in the temple architecture. The temple was also the god's house, with reception, sleeping and storage areas*

Fig. 18 *The Temple of Amun at Karnak. Generally the priesthood in Egypt was a part-time occupation, the priests serving in the temple on a rotational basis. However, because of its size and importance, some priests at Karnak would have been permanent personnel. Most would have lived within or near the temple precinct*

groups of lay priests who carried out the religious services for the god: each group had the same number of people and distribution of functions and served, on a rotational basis, for only three months in a year. The group's temple duty lasted for one month on each occasion, and there was a three-month period between each term of office when the priests were free to pursue their lives and other careers (often as scribes, doctors or lawyers) outside the temple. They could marry and, outside their period of temple duty, they lived with their families.

The word used for the ordinary level of temple priest was 'wāāb' (Natsef-Amun held this along with other titles), which meant that the individual had attained a certain physical purity which allowed him to enter the god's presence and to have contact with the deity's possessions. Herodotus again provides details of these purification requirements; he says that the priests 'bathe in cold water twice a day and twice a night – and observe innumerable ceremonies besides.' These ablutions were usually performed in the sacred lake found inside most temple enclosures, before the priest entered the temple building. He also cleansed his mouth with natron, and both purifications were based on the god's own toilet which was performed daily in the rituals, emphasizing how the use of water symbolized rebirth and rejuvenation.

Other requirements are also given in Herodotus: 'The priests shave their bodies all over every day to guard against the presence of lice, or anything else equally unpleasant, while they are about their religious duties', and 'They circumcise themselves for cleanliness' sake, preferring to be clean rather than comely.' This ceremony was probably performed once they had entered the priesthood; adult male circumcision was practised in ancient Egypt, although it was not a universal custom there, and is shown in wall scenes in the tomb of Ankhmahor at Saqqara.

Although the priests could marry, they were expected to practise sexual abstinence during their term of office in the temple, and Herodotus states: 'It was the Egyptians who first made it an offence against piety to have intercourse with women in temples or to enter there after having intercourse without having previously washed.' Several days of abstinence from contact with women were required before the priest could undertake his duties in the temple.

There were certain prohibitions with regard to their clothes; according to Herodotus, 'they wear linen only and shoes made from the papyrus plant – these materials, for dress and shoes, being the only ones allowed them.' They were forbidden to wear clothes made from materials that came from living animals (such as wool or leather), in case such contact should contaminate the purity of the god's sanctuary. The fine linen garment worn by the priest changed little in style over the centuries, preserving the original features found in the Old Kingdom; it also differed only in detail to indicate the owner's exact priestly function, and truly distinctive apparel was reserved for the high priests and officiants in special categories.

Some foods were also forbidden to the priest. Herodotus claims that they could not touch fish or beans, but other Classical writers list a whole variety of prohibited items, including pork, lamb, beef, pigeon and garlic. It is most probable that these varied from one location to another, so that the priests of one region were prevented from eating the meat of the cult animal or the sacred plant associated with their particular god, whereas this prohibition did not apply elsewhere.

Often it is only the name of a priest and his list of titles that are known to us, and although the temples were the largest employers of personnel in Egypt, the exact organization of the staff and the duties and functions performed by the various title-holders are still not clear. The Temple of Amun at Karnak was a vast institution, but generally the temples had three categories of employees. First, there were the senior priests, including those who came into direct contact with the god's cult statue when they performed the daily rituals. This group also contained the specialists who were employed in the House of Life; these institutions probably adjoined all the major temples and were centres where the sacred wisdom of the divine cult was perpetuated, and where the texts which could adorn the temple walls and be written in the papyri were composed and copied. The Egyptians greatly valued the ability to read and write hieroglyphs, since they believed that the sacred texts contained the ancient wisdom which was in turn the key source of cosmic power. In the House of Life, the scholarly scribes would discuss and develop the god's theology and mythology, and compile the protective magical incantations and funerary texts, in addition to the astronomical tables that were needed in their work. The Greeks called these scribe-scholars 'Hierogrammatists', and Classical writers acknowledged their great wisdom and knowledge. Some were members of the priesthood, but there were also lay specialists, experts in the fields of medicine (many of the Medical Papyri would have been composed here), the use of plants, geography, the history of the Egyptian kings, astrology and astronomy. It was probably in the House of Life that instruction was given in a wide variety of subjects, and perhaps medical students received some of their training here.

The second group of temple personnel were the minor clergy. These were probably regarded as assistants in the various religious activities and would have been engaged in many tasks such as carrying the sacred barque containing the god's statue when it left the temple, and supervising employees engaged to decorate and renovate the temple. Even these men, however, would have undergone a selection and initiation process and would have met the requirement of being ritually pure.

The third category was the auxiliary staff who were not priests; they were needed so that the temple, its lands, estates and workshops could function properly, and they included architects, painters and sculptors, doorkeepers and guards, estate workers who grew the food, craftsmen who made the utensils used in the divine rituals, and the butchers, bakers, confectioners and florists engaged in preparing the god's daily offerings. There were also large numbers of people who ensured that the temple was a clean and fitting residence for the deity.

In the villages of predynastic Egypt, reed shrines had once housed and protected the statues of the gods. Later these developed into the great stone temples, but, being a conservative people who retained the beliefs and customs that had always served them well, the Egyptians chose to preserve and retain the main architectural and ritual features of the earliest reed shrines. Eventually, two types of temple developed from the shrines: these were the so-called cultus temple (such as Karnak) where the daily services were performed by the high priest, as the king's delegate, on behalf of the resident god; and the mortuary temple, which was originally attached to the royal burial place as in the pyramid complex. However, in the New Kingdom, these temples were separate buildings where rituals were performed not only on behalf of the great state god but also for all the previous legitimate rulers (the Royal Ancestors) and particularly for the king who had built the temple, so that he might enjoy eternity as a divine ruler. Rituals, performed daily and following the same pattern in all the mortuary temples throughout Egypt, provided for the welfare of the god and the Ancestors and, in return, sought benefits from them for the king and his people.

In the cultus temple, the priests performed the divine ritual three times daily; it took the form of wakening, washing, dressing, feeding and returning to his shrine the god's statue. In the mortuary temples, in an additional ritual, the food was removed from the god's altar and presented to the Royal Ancestors. The essence of the food was believed to sustain the spirit of the god and of the Ancestors, but physically of course the food was still there at the conclusion of the rituals, and it was then taken outside the temple and divided among the priests as their regular wages. Some priests were apparently sufficiently unscrupulous to eat the food without first offering it up to the god!

The temple deity, in addition to the daily attention, also enjoyed periods of rest and recreation which were provided in the form of festivals. These varied from place to place, and were held at different times of the year, but they were all times of great rejoicing, each re-enacting special events in a particular

Fig. 19 *A wall-scene in the Temple of Amun at Karnak, showing a procession of priests carrying the sacred barque. This held the cult statue of the god, which was paraded outside the temple during the great festivals. This provided the ordinary people with their only opportunity of standing in the god's presence*

god's mythology. A portable statue of the deity was carried outside the temple precinct by the priests, and such processions, accompanied by chanting and incense-burning, passed among the crowds, giving them their only opportunity to participate in the god's cult. It was usual for such events to attract large numbers of pilgrims to the god's town.

The temple was the 'god's mansion', a place of extreme sanctity where the divinity could reside in his statue or cult animal and be approached by the priests (the king's delegates) on behalf of the country. However, each temple was also regarded as the original 'Island of Creation', the place where the mythology stated that all the elements of life and civilization had first come into existence. Each temple was considered to be the place of creation, a centre of great spiritual potency where the divine force could reach mankind, and thus it was essential to recreate the landscape of the original Island in every temple building. This was achieved with gradually inclining floor levels, soaring plant columns and capitals, and a ceiling decorated as the sky, so that, by means of magic, the temple could be 'brought to life' to become the fertile Island of Creation.

The magnitude of the Egyptian temple can be seen in its most extreme form in the great complex of buildings known today as Karnak. Here there is a confusing spectacle of courtyards,

Fig. 20 *The Temple of Luxor, dedicated to the goddess Mut, who was the consort of Amun. This temple, a short distance from Amun's temple complex at Karnak, was Mut's residence and received the cult statue of Amun when he made his annual visit to Mut*

colonnades, obelisks and pylons, since, started in the 12th Dynasty, this complex was altered and expanded many times by different rulers who all wanted to leave their mark at Karnak. This most sacred site incorporates several main buildings; the largest is the Temple of Amun (Amen-Re), approached down an avenue of ram-headed sphinxes and divided internally into several sections by six great pylons (gateways). Another avenue of pylons leads off to the nearby temple of Amun's wife, Mut, and the complex also includes a temple dedicated to their son, Khonsu. The gods Ptah and Montu also had temples within the enclosure. These were originally separate sanctuaries which were eventually included in Amun's complex and brought under the supervision of his priesthood so that they would not rival his supremacy at Thebes. These complicated arrangements at Karnak explain why Natsef-Amun had several functions here and why he was both 'Scribe in the Shrine of Montu' and 'Scribe of the Sacred Bulls of Amun, Mut and Khonsu.'

The Temple of Amun at Karnak employed thousands of people, and by the New Kingdom could boast a larger staff than the king himself. In the reign of Ramesses III, according to Papyrus Harris, it had more than 80,000 employees and owned more than 2000 square kilometres of land. The personnel had as many as 125 different functions, and the priesthood of Amun became far more powerful than any other group in Egypt. At Karnak, the most important post was that of High Priest of Amun; the holder, known as the First Prophet of Amun, enjoyed extensive powers and owned a great house and estates. Next in rank were the Fathers of the God who included the Second, Third and Fourth Prophets of Amun. Promotion through this hierarchy was usually by a system of progressive selection, so that, in time, they would all hope to advance. Below them were the *waāb* priests ('the purified') who had less elevated duties, and, as in other temples, there were lay workers who included stewards, clerks, police, and the overseers of the estates and granaries.

The priests of Amun had not always wielded such economic and political power. In the 12th Dynasty, the cult of the local god Amun began to develop at Thebes and, when local rulers became the kings of Egypt, they adopted and promoted this god as their royal patron deity. In the 18th Dynasty, when the Theban princes drove out the Hyksos and established themselves as kings, they further enhanced the god's wealth and reputation in thanks for the victory he had given them; with the later conquests in Syria/Palestine, the gifts of tribute and booty to Amen-Re increased. In effect, these kings were guilty of creating an all-powerful dynastic deity whose ambitious clergy were soon to become a 'state within a state' and to rival the king's own power. One example of this is the way in which the post of Chief of the Prophets of the North and South came into their control. Originally, this had been held by the vizier, the chief state official, who used this position to affirm the king's supremacy over the gods on earth and their priests. Now, however, it was taken over by the high priest of Amun, enabling him to promote his god's cult still further. These men also wielded considerable power in the great assemblies to which the temples all sent priest representatives to present their views to the king on many common problems, including the temple taxes, revenues, repairs and extensions. The most important right exercised by the high priest of Amun, however, was to confer or withhold the god's approval of the choice of the royal heir.

From the reign of Tuthmosis III (1504–1450 BC) onwards, the priests of Amun reached their zenith, so that the later kings gradually attempted to throw off this stranglehold and to redress the balance. They married outside the royal family, thwarting the priests' support of the traditional consanguineous royal union and influence on the succession; and they began to promote the old sun god as a rival, culminating in Akhenaten's advancement of the Aten cult and the so-called Amarna revolution.

The Ramesside rulers of the 19th Dynasty emphasized their allegiance to a multiplicity of gods, thus curtailing Amun's excessive power. This family originated in the Delta, and they developed the northern religious centres while continuing the worship of Amun at Thebes. However, the effective kings who ruled at the beginning of this dynasty were succeeded by later Ramessides whose political weakness allowed the priests of Amun to gain ascendancy once again. In the reign of Ramesses XI they attempted to seize supreme power. Although they did not succeed, their actions divided the country, and they remained virtually in control of the south. It was only under the dynamic kings of the 25th and 26th Dynasties that the political status of the king was restored. These men installed their daughters at Thebes as Divine Wives of Amun so that they had supreme power in the city and the surrounding district, thus effectively thwarting the ambitions of the high priests of Amun.

Natsef-Amun lived in the troubled times of the late 20th Dynasty, in the reign of Ramesses XI, and was employed at Karnak when Herihor, as High Priest of Amun, wielded unprecedented political power. It would have been a time of intrigue, and Natsef-Amun was doubtless politically shrewd and ambitious. According to the Leeds archive, he was married to the daughter of one of the highest functionaries at the Memnonium (Karnak), Amenemtephis, whose grandson (a son of Natsef-Amun) later succeeded him there. His family obviously followed the tradition of obtaining the priesthood through inheritance.

At Karnak Natsef-Amun held a number of priestly offices. He probably participated in the divine offering rituals. Relatively tall and with a commanding presence, he would have undertaken his temple duties with dignity as he passed, shaven-headed and attired in the priest's white linen garments, along the processional routes through the darkened halls and chambers of Amun's temple. Above him, the plant-form columns soared to the roof and ahead of him, through the wafting incense that he sometimes carried, there was the sanctuary where the god's statue rested. At the completion of the daily service, Natsef-Amun would have joined his fellow-priests in dividing and eating the food brought from the god's altar. His other duties took him to the nearby temple of Montu, the ancient god of war, and, as a scribe, he may also have spent time in the House of Life, composing and copying texts. There would also have been inventories, reports and administrative documents to complete in connection with his role as Scribe of the Accounts of the Cattle of the Estate of Amun. His main duty here was to record the quantity of corn offered to and consumed by the Sacred Cattle, and this would have formed part of the lists which were meticulously kept at the temple. The Sacred Cattle were destined for the god's daily banquet, and had to be selected and killed according to specific religious regulations, to ensure their ritual purity. A specialized priest supervised the ceremony of slaughter, symbolically striking the chosen animal and, once it had been butchered, declaring that it was ritually pure. According to some texts, these ritual executors were personnel of the House of Life. To select an animal for slaughter, the priest had to inspect the cattle and be able to recognize particular physical signs. According to Herodotus, if the priest found that the animal had 'even a single black hair upon him, [he] pronounces him unclean', and an inspection had to be made of the tongue and the tail, to 'make sure that the hair on it grows properly'.

Natsef-Amun lived at a time when Egypt's boundaries had narrowed considerably. His city of Thebes was no longer the cosmopolitan centre of world events that it had once been. Herihor and his descendants, powerful in this locality, were nevertheless politically weak compared with earlier rulers and they lacked any national authority. We can only guess that Natsef-Amun, a successful man within this confined world, was himself somewhat introverted and parochial in attitude. At least outwardly he must have supported his high priest, the ambitious Herihor, but it was the name of his king, Ramesses XI – who still held supreme power – that was inscribed on the leather ornament placed within the wrappings of his mummy.

6 Mummies in Leeds Museums

P.C.D. Brears

The first scholar in Leeds to take any interest in Egyptology was the town's great local historian and collector, Ralph Thoresby (1658–1725). On 26 January 1709, while on a visit to London, he was shown round the private museum of John Kempt (1665–1717), where the proud owner displayed 'two entire mummies, (in their wooden chests, shaped with a human head &c, one of which has the Egyptian hieroglyphics painted upon the swathing-bands; he had fragments of another, and gave me a piece . . .)' (Brears, 1989). Having brought this prize specimen back to his own 'Museum Thoresbyanum' in Leeds, Thoresby proceeded to describe it in his *Ducatus Leodiensis* (1715):

> A Fragment of an Egyptian Mummy, the Flesh converted into a Sort of black Rosin by the Oils or Gums used at the embalming, which hath so incorporated it self, that the very innermost Part of the Bones are of as black a Colour as if burnt, Here are also Samples of three different sorts of Linen Cloths, wherein it was wrapped, each of deeper tincture than [the] other, the outermost painted with Blue.

After Thoresby's death in 1725, the majority of his collections 'having lain in a garret like a Heap of Rubbish from 1726 to 1743, the rain, snow, etc. beating in on all sides, and during that time several persons rummaging them underfoot, so they became like a Dunghill' were either 'thrown on the Dunghill', used to repair the highways, or were sold off as scrap. It would appear that his mummy fragment was destroyed at this time, for it is not listed among the small number of items subsequently rescued and sold off (Brears and Davies, 1989).

Over the succeeding century, local interest in Egypt appears to have been confined to its role as a battlefield between Napoleon's forces which invaded it in 1798, and the British army which invaded it in 1801. In 1827, the catalogue of the fashionable Leeds Library listed only two books on Egypt, these being J. P. Morier's *Memoirs of a Campaign in Egypt* (1801) and General Sir Robert T. Wilson's *History of the Expedition to Egypt* (1802).

After the Napoleonic Wars, with the threat of invasion effectively removed and the local economy flourishing, Leeds' scientific, manufacturing and commercial community came together to form a Philosophical and Literary Society in 1818. This was to discuss and promote 'all the Branches of Natural Knowledge and Literature, but excluding all topics of Religion, Politics, and Ethics'. Backed by the wealthiest families in the town, the society rapidly accumulated sufficient funds to erect a fine Greek Revival Philosophical Hall. Opened in 1821, it featured a large lecture hall, a library, meeting rooms, a well-appointed museum, and a laboratory. There was one salaried post of sub-curator, but membership of the council of management and other curatorial posts were entirely honorary, being occupied by local professional men. This whole venture proved so successful that the museum galleries had to be greatly enlarged in 1825 in order to accommodate the ever increasing number of fine specimens.

Fig. 21 *The Philosophical Hall, Leeds. Erected in 1819–21 to the designs of R.D. Chantrell, it was one of Britain's first purpose-built museums*

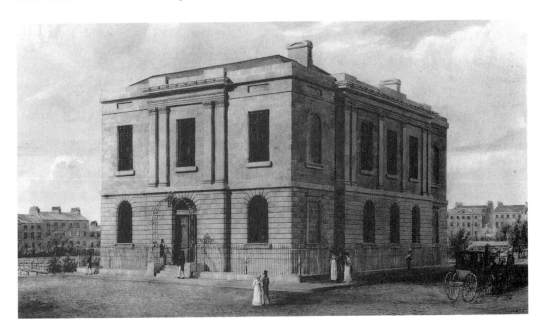

On 2 February 1824, the *Leeds Intelligencer* reported: 'We understand that a Mummy procured from Thebes in the autumn of 1822 by Mr Salt, his Britannic Majesty's Consul-General in Egypt, has been presented to the Society by Wm. Maude Esq.' Henry Salt was perhaps the central figure in the exploration of ancient Egypt at this time; not only did he carry out his own investigations, but he also used a number of field workers, including the famous Giovanni Belzoni (see page 13) and Giovanni Athanasi (a Greek) to loot the ruins of Upper Egypt to procure suitable antiquities. These he sold to major institutions such as the British Museum and the French government. (Wortham, 1971)

When this mummy was subsequently investigated by John Atkinson, the curator, and William Osburn, the secretary, they were able to inform the readers of the *Leeds Intelligencer* for 17 March 1825 that it was

Fig. 22 *John Atkinson, Curator of the Leeds Museum from 1818 to 1828. He worked with Osburn on the translation of the hieroglyphics on the Leeds mummies*

> probably from one or other of the Catacombes of Lower Egypt. – The case has contained the body of a man who seems to have been a soldier – The military caste in Egypt was quite distinct from all others; the privilege of possessing lands was entirely confined to it, and to the priests. His name was 'Pethor' which means 'the Votary of Horus', a god in high esteem among the Egyptian soldiers. The four leading inscriptions on this case commence with the formula:– 'This is the body of the Osirian [An epithet of dead persons] Lord Pethor deceased: the son of Enthaout (or Harnthaout), deceased; his mother was the Lady Thetisi, deceased'. The remaining part of the inscriptions, as well as the decorations on the case, are mythological, and relate to the opinions entertained by the Egyptians concerning the soul after death. The mummy which this case contained presented no remarkable appearance when opened. The linen which was abundantly enveloped was of a uniform texture; and from the powerful odour of asphaltum or mineral pitch that was emitted, it had probably been embalmed according to the third method mentioned by Herodotus. The skin and flesh of the body had been almost entirely consumed by a small brown beetle, of which numerous were found in a perfect state among the folds of the linen. This curious circumstance had not, I believe, been noticed before.

From this account, it is clear that the honorary officers of the Leeds Philosophical and Literary Society had acquired considerable knowledge of Egyptology, including the remarkable ability to read hieroglyphics. In fact, they had been able to assemble an extremely competent research team of very able young and enthusiastic professional men.

Fig. 23 *Thomas Pridgin Teale, surgeon, was responsible for carrying out the 'thorough anatomical examination' of Natsef-Amun in 1824–5*

Their leader was William Osburn (1793–1875), son of a wine merchant in Upperhead Row, who had been educated first by Dr Hamilton in Chapeltown, and then at Leeds Grammar School, before he entered his father's business. A founder member of the society, and its secretary from 1825 to 1829, he also conducted classes at St Paul's Sunday School, Park Square.

The second member of the team was John Atkinson FLS (1787–1828), son of the vicar of St Paul's. On leaving Leeds Grammar School he had become the pupil of the great Leeds surgeon William Hey, then practising both on his own account and as Surgeon to the Lying-in Hospital in Leeds from 1824. Also a founder member of the Society, he had been appointed its first curator in 1818.

The third member, chiefly responsible for the anatomical reports, was Thomas Pridgin Teale FRCS, FRS, Hon MD (1801–1867). Educated at Heath Grammar School, Wakefield, and the Leeds Grammar School, he had become the pupil of his father, Thomas Teale, surgeon, before studying in Edinburgh, London and Paris. He was assisted by the fourth member, Richard C. Hey, a relation of William Hey, who was Surgeon to the Leeds Eye Dispensary.

The fifth member was Edward Sanderson George FLS (1801–1830), son of Thomas George, stuff dyer and finisher of Spring Gardens, Kirkstall Road. As a member of his father's company, he brought considerable skills in organic chemistry as practised in the dyeworks.

Finally there was Henry Denny FRMS, ALS (1803–1871) who moved to Leeds from Norwich in 1825 in order to become the society's first professional sub-curator. Among his many skills Denny was an exquisite biological draughtsman, well able to prepare the lithographic stones required for printing the final plates of illustrations.

While this team was coming together, a second mummy, that of the priest Natsef-Amun, had slowly been transported from Egypt towards Leeds. M. J. Passalacqua, 'a most successful spoliator of the tombs of the ancient Egyptians', had sent two remarkably finely preserved mummies from Gournor, the cemetery for Thebes, to his native town of Trieste at the head of the Adriatic in 1823. These, he believed, had then been sent on to London (Osburn, 1828, I). In November 1823, Mr William Bullock, the great showman and dealer in antiquities, had returned to his famous Egyptian Hall in Piccadilly after a year's collecting in Mexico (Attick, 1978). Back in London, he had purchased what was apparently one of Passalacqua's mummies from a gentleman who had brought it into England as a speculation.

Presumably it was Atkinson and Osburn who persuaded John

Blayds (1754–1827), a wealthy banker of Park House, Leeds, and Oulton Hall, Oulton, to purchase this fine specimen for the society's museum, where it would undoubtedly help to further their studies. The details of the mummy's acquisition were announced in the *Leeds Intelligencer* in 1824:

EGYPTIAN MUMMY

An Egyptian Mummy, in high preservation, and enclosed in a most elaborately ornamented case, has been presented to the Philosophical Society of this town, by the liberality of John Blayds, Esq. This specimen appears to have been selected with great care, from a small collection at Bullock's Museum, with the assistance of Dr. Noehdin, one of the Antiquarian Conservators of the British Museum and W. Roscoe, Esq. late of Liverpool. It appears from the emblems, with which it is associated, to be a priest, under the envelope of which papyrus is generally found. Mr W. B. Hudson, who effected the purchase of this valuable curiosity, says, that he is quite satisfied that it is a genuine Egyptian Mummy, of a very rare kind, and that it is in very fine preservation. Mr. Bullock is of the opinion that there is not a finer in the British Museum. The gentleman who brought it to England bought it on speculation, and is a loser by it. A few years ago an inferior mummy sold at Plymouth for £300. We congratulate the Philosophical Society on the acquisition of this splendid relic of antiquity, which will prove a conspicuous ornament, and a powerful attractive of their increasing collection.

Later the council of the society praised John Blayds for his gift of this 'excellent Specimen, of that wonderful art, which, though itself extinct, has conferred a Species of immortality on the only perishable parts of human Nature.' Early in September 1824, the council decided that this mummy should be opened in the presence of both themselves and Mr Blayds. Work proceeded throughout the following winter, and by 17 March 1825 Osburn was able to publish an introductory account of the unwrapping in the pages of the *Leeds Intelligencer*.

Having lifted the lid of the coffin, with its splendid hieroglyphics and decorations, they found an inner lid,

made of some light wood (probably cedar), which rests upon the mummy, and which is evidently intended to represent the white garment of the initiated. The mask on this lid is well preserved, and represents a physiognomy by no means devoid of interest

Then came the mummy itself,

enveloped in linen of two kinds. The coarser quality is about equal to that which would be bought in the town at 12*d*., and the finer at 2*s*. 2*d*. This linen has evidently formed a part of the dress of the deceased, during his lifetime; it is worn in many places, and has been repaired by the process usually called *darning*. After removing about fourteen folds of linen, a wreath of natural flowers and berries was found on the breast . . . When the unwrapping had proceeded a little further, a lotus flower was discovered over the head and face, in exactly the same position as those represented on the masks on the case . . . This was not, as the others, a natural flower; but has been made artificially of some unknown substance. . . .

Finally the body itself was revealed, perfectly preserved, and 'thickly covered with pounded spices'. 'A thorough anatomical examination' was carried out by Teale and Hey, while samples of the human tissue, the gum from the bandages, and the spicery (largely myrrh and cassia) were carefully analyzed by George. The translation of the hieroglyphics, meanwhile, was completed by Atkinson and Osburn.

In 1823, when the first mummy arrived in Leeds, the secret of translating the lost hieroglyphic script of the ancient Egyptians was just being rediscovered after centuries of fruitless surmise. The key had been provided by the discovery of the Rosetta Stone near the town of Rashid on the western arm of the Nile in 1801. It was inscribed with three inscriptions identical in content, firstly in hieroglyphics, secondly in Greek, and thirdly in demotic, a cursive later Egyptian script. Dr Thomas Young (1773–1829) a fine physicist and linguist, was the first scholar to translate the demotic inscription, and in 1815–16 he had translated the name of the foreign rulers in the hieroglyphics. These discoveries, together with Young's further views, were read by Osburn in the *Encyclopedia Britannica* of 1819.

Within a few years Young's very considerable achievements were being eclipsed by those of Jean Francois Champollion (1790–1832). His major discoveries regarding the predominantly phonetic nature of hieroglyphic script were published in 1822, and in the spring of 1824 his *Précis du Système Hiéroglyphique* gave interpretations of royal names, words and phrases, and even complete sentences.

This was the tool which enabled Atkinson and Osburn to translate the inscriptions on their mummies, and to present a series of six lectures 'On the Hieroglyphical Antiquities of Egypt' in January and February 1825. Here the members of the society were able to discover how, 'By the industry of these Gentlemen, the modern discoveries of Champollion and Young were applied apparently with considerable success to the interpretation of the inscriptions covering the cases of these Remarkable Relics.'

In January 1827, the council gave Osburn permission to purchase the Catalogue of the Papyri in the Vatican, and also to contact Dr Young, as secretary and founder of the Syro-Egyptian Society, in order to obtain their published plates of hieroglyphics. Having received a suitable reply from the Royal Society of Literature, who were now publishing the Syro-Egyptian Society's works, it was agreed that six fascicules should be purchased for the sum of twelve guineas. In addition, Mr F. T. Bilham purchased a cast of the Rosetta Stone from the British Museum in 1826 in order to help the work.

Work now proceeded in earnest to prepare the results of the mummy team's researches for publication, Henry Denny carefully drawing elevations of the mummy case, the leather ornaments, hieroglyphic inscriptions and the internal organs in fine and accurate detail. All was completed in June 1828, when the sixty-page *An Account of an Egyptian Mummy presented to the Museum of the Leeds Philosophical and Literary Society* (Osburn, 1828 II) was received from Robinson and Hernaman, the Leeds printers, and offered for sale to both the membership and the public at large. It was a model publication for its period, the quality of the descriptions of the unwrapping, the details of the decorative features, the translation of the hieroglyphics, the anatomical and chemical examinations all representing the highest possible standards. It still stands as a remarkable tribute to the standards of scholarship achieved by the provincial Philosophical museums of the early nineteenth century.

By the time this report was published, John Blayds had already died, in 1827. John Atkinson, the curator, died in October 1828, and was followed by Edward Sanderson George in February 1830. Of the other members of the team, Henry Denny continued to develop the Leeds Museum until it was second to none in provincial England, dying in office in 1871, while Thomas Teale followed a very distinguished career as a Leeds surgeon and co-founder of the Leeds Medical School, dying in 1867. William Osburn went on to study Egyptology in greater detail, presenting lectures on 'Egyptian Mummies' in 1826–7, and on 'The System of Numerical Notation and on the Calendar of the Ancient Egyptians', 'The Origin of Written Characters' and 'Hieroglyphics' in 1828–9. After a short period as a tutor to the sons of Lord Wriothesley Russell at Chenies, he became tutor to the sons of Sir John Paul in 1847, travelling with them to Egypt and Ceylon.

His output of books became quite prolific during the period between 1835 and 1857 when he published eight titles. Reviews criticized his work unmercifully, since he claimed that the scenes on the walls of the Egyptian monuments contained proof that the Israelites had lived in Egypt for a long period. He also refused to accept Champollion's account of the evolution of the Egyptian system of writing, denied that the Hyksos invasion had ever taken place, and declared Manetho's list of kings to be completely unreliable – conclusions that no contemporary Egyptologist would accept. He saw Israelites on Egyptian monuments where no one else had been able to do so, and he announced that an intimate relationship existed between the ancient Egyptian and the Hebrew languages. Finally, he believed that the Egyptians had originally resided on the plains of Babel and that Cheops had raised the Great Pyramid as a faint imitation of that famous tower that was to reach to heaven.

Despite the eccentricity of these views, his books enjoyed excellent sales. He died at New Wortley, Leeds, in February 1875, his memorial window at the east end of St Edmunds' Church, Providence Street, The Bank, Leeds, featuring the appropriately Christian/Egyptian theme of 'The Flight into Egypt'.

In addition to these members, one other person was involved in the mummy project. He was John Marshall (1765–1845), head of the Leeds flax-spinning industry, and one of Britain's major industrial magnates. A founder member of the Philosophical and Literary Society, he provided it with extensive financial support and served as its first president from 1819 to 1826, when he entered Parliament. As president, he chaired all the council and lecture meetings, and would have been present at the unwrapping of the mummy. This experience appears to have made a considerable impression on him, for when he and his son decided to build a new flax mill in Holbeck in 1838–40, they commissioned the Egyptian specialist Joseph Bonomi to design its façades in the form of a great Egyptian temple. Using his unrivalled knowledge of the temples of Karnak, Edfu and Philae, which he had studied between 1824 and 1834, and massive blocks of the local Bramley Fall gritstone, Bonomi created a building which has continued to astound and impress all visitors to industrial South Leeds up to the present day. There are many descriptions of its two-acre spinning mill, its ornate office block with papyrus columns, and its chimney (now demolished) in the form of a giant Cleopatra's Needle. Of these, the following colourfully recreates a first impression of 1849:

> Behold the huge black monster of a mill, how it crouches there . . . I honour thy mighty walls as the framework of the truest modern temple of God and his worship. What were Osiris and Iris to Marshall Brothers?

What was the music of the Memnon Statue at sunrise, to

the melody and world-wide, heaven-high, and hell-deep significance of the factory bell at cock-crowing? O! how unspeakably beautiful and terrible are the troops of Factory Girls. Surprised out of sleep . . . they become shrieking oracles of the divine, and rushing into the mill-caves, their inner prophecies take tangible shape in living accomplished work . . . in Marshall's two acre sanctuary . . . each awful sister like a Nemesis, her black hair streaming over her shoulders . . . or bound up in picturesque turbans, some stained in bloody vermilion, and others steeped in the dyeing vats of the Tyrian purple – doing her appointed work.

Gaze now upon the frontal entrance to the temple, what a religious aspect it presents; severely pillared and fretted with ornaments. The serpent of the Egyptians rears its sacred head in an entablature over the doorway. No ghostly pageantry of priests, – worshippers of Onions, Crocadiles and Bulls – now passes its lintels; yet as the dead die not, but live forever. I see Holbeck transformed to Memphis, and the festival of Theophania celebrated in its streets. There go the priests of Apis! leading the sacred bull in solemn procession through the streets followed by crowds of rejoicing devotees with emblematic banners, and preceded by a chorus of swarthy children singing his honours!

(Phillips, 1849)

Fig. 24 *Painted by W.B. Robinson in 1849, this watercolour effectively captures the scale and majesty of Marshall and Company's vast Egyptian flax mill in Holbeck, Leeds. It was built to the designs of Joseph Bonomi in 1838–40*

Even in his most profound thoughts, Natsef-Amun could never have imagined that he would eventually be responsible for the building of a great Egyptian temple in the heart of a West Riding industrial suburb, three thousand years after his life had ended.

The mummy of Natsef-Amun had been placed on exhibition on the first floor of the museum in a large glass case costing ten pounds. It was described in the 1854 guidebook as the mummy of Ensa-Amoun: 'From the inscription on the walls of the tomb in which he was interred near Gournon, it appears that he was married to a daughter of Amenemtephis, one of the highest functionaries of the Memnomium; the latter died at the age of 88, and was succeeded in his sacred office by his grandson, a son of Ensa-Amoun.'

In the 1860s one Timothy Goorkrodger, a typical inhabitant of the Pennine textile valleys of West Yorkshire, recorded his opinion of this notable antiquity:

> There's a mummy, as they calls it – a sort of pickled body from Egypt – where they keep their dead relashuns in great caves and peerhymeeds, instead of buryin' of 'em as we do . . . Lady standin' by said she's never seen a mummy with grander painting and gilding on it, Lady said too, 'Them Egyptshun priests war main cunnin' clever fellos, and they made millions upon millions believe in 'em for ages. Who believes in 'em noo? Not a soul!' says she. Them Egyptshuns mun have been queer foaks to pickle each other in this fashion; The funny thing is they pickled cats and crokadyles, and other varmints the same way. They mun have had plenty of vinegar, I think, and lots of spare time in them old days!
>
> (Fetherston, *c*.1870)

Over the years, further mummy specimens were acquired from a variety of sources. In 1849, for example Messrs. Thomas and Cooper Fenteman, new and old booksellers, dealers in prints, carvings and curiosities at 13 Duncan Street and 42 Boar Lane, 'liberally presented an Egyptian Mummy and Coffin, and although the body is not in so good a state of preservation as to admit of its exhibition, the case illustrates the state of the art in that country at a different period from either of those in the Museum, and is, consequently, possessed of much interest' (Slade and Roebuck, 1851).

It was most probably this mummy that brought with it its own 'passport', a large handmade paper Turkish firman of the Grand Seignor, now in the museum collections, which permitted the vessel carrying the mummy to pass the forts of the Dardanelles. It is dated AH 1221, that is 1801 AD. This would suggest that both the mummy and the firman were on board ship probably with the straw-stuffed heads of recently killed Marmelukes ready to be brought back to Constantinople at the time of the Egyptian wars between the Turks and the Marmelukes. The fact that the mummy and the firman remained together, for which there was no administrative reason, further suggests that this journey was never completed, but that they were captured by the British Expeditionary Force at Alexandria some time between its arrival in March 1807 and its departure the following September. Having returned to England, they presumably entered a private collection before being acquired by the Fentemans.

In 1862, Mr G. Morley presented 'Two Heads and the Foot of a Mummy and Two Mummies of the Ibis . . . from Egypt' while Mr John Holmes contributed the bulk of the subscription required for 'the valuable acquisition of a Peruvian Mummy'. To these the Rev. J. Ridley of Brownhill Vicarage, Birstall, added 'The Mummied foot of a lady from Thebes' of the 18th–21st dynasty in 1896.' In the following year Mr H. Bendelack Hewetson, surgeon, of 12 Hanover Square, Leeds, gave his personal collection of antiquities to the museum. They included 'two beautiful examples of mummy cases, mounted in an upright glazed case of ebonised wood, a mummy hand, and a cat mummy' probably from Old Alexandria.

In the Philosophical and Literary Society's lecture programme for 1894–5, the famous Egyptologist Professor W. M. Flinders Petrie presented a paper on 'A New Race in Egypt'. After giving the museum a very valuable selection of alabaster and clay-baked vessels used by the New Race, which he had discovered in the Libyan Desert between Ballas and Nagada, he inspected the mummy of Natsef-Amun. Having read the hieroglyphics, he deduced that the case alone belonged to this priest of the time of Amenhotep III (1400 BC), the mummy being that of a later interloper, who had died in the reign of Ramesses XII, (1070 BC). Regrettably these opinions were incorrect, confusing the mummy's status and identity for much of the following century.

From the 1860s the mummy was displayed in the centre of the outer vestibule, where it stood 'just within the door of the hall, exposed on one side to the inrush of air from the street and on the other to the heat from the fire [which is not] well chosen for the preservation of the fragile remains.' To remedy this situation, a fine new case was constructed in 1931–2 which displayed the upper lid, the inner lid, and the open mummy case one above the other, along with the internal organs. Fortunately it was not replaced in its former position, for this was where a high explosive bomb scored a direct hit in the air raid of 15 March 1941. As it was, the blast appears to have been considerable, pounding through the glass case, shattering the inner lid, and covering the mummy in broken glass, dust and debris.

Fig. 25 *Here the outer and inner lids, the glazed coffin, and the viscera are seen in their new case made in 1931–2. The blast from the 1941 bomb punched directly through the large sheets of plate glass, smashing the inner lid, but fortunately leaving Natsef-Amun and his outer coffin largely unscathed*

Almost miraculously, the outer mummy case and its contents sustained little permanent damage. The other mummies were not so fortunate, however, all of them apparently being destroyed. Even today, stories still circulate of fragments of mummy being found scattered in the street outside the museum by early morning passers-by.

After the war, the mummy of Natsef-Amun was displayed in the large zoological gallery, the surviving section of the old museum building, before being transferred to its present home in the new City Museum premises in the Municipal Buildings, Park Row, in 1967–9.

Within the present century, the City Museum has continued

to use the most modern research methods to discover more about this mummy. In 1931–2 for example, Dr A. J. E. Cave of Leeds University School of Medicine carried out an x-ray examination. From this, he discovered that Natsef-Amun had probably suffered from either fever or a dietetic disturbance at some time during his life, but that he was not suffering from any fractures, disease, or joint troubles when he died in middle age. Further x-ray examinations undertaken in 1964 by M. L. Lehmann of the University of Sheffield School of Dentistry revealed that his teeth were in very poor condition, a number being missing, while the remainder were badly worn down and over-erupted from the jaw.

Over the past decades, the techniques of mummy investigation have made great advances, especially since the inauguration of the Manchester Egyptian Mummy Research Project at the Manchester Museum in 1973. This multidisciplinary team, led by Dr Rosalie David, has recovered new information about the occurrence of disease, causes of death, dietary habits, living conditions and funerary beliefs and customs in ancient Egypt. When the Leeds City Museum decided in 1989 that Natsef-Amun should benefit from these advances, it was obvious, therefore, that it should turn to the Manchester Project to carry out the necessary research.

7 The Manchester Mummy Project

A.R. David

When the Curator of Egyptology at Manchester Museum, Miss Winifred Crompton, was asked in 1925 why Manchester came to have one of Britain's most important collections of Egyptian antiquities, she replied:

> It is due to the interest taken by one Manchester man, the late Dr. Jesse Haworth, in ancient Egypt. For years, he financed the excavations of Professor Petrie. After the results of his work had aroused public interest all over the country, excavation societies were formed whose members subscribed to the work. The most important of these are the British School of Archaeology in Egypt, directed by Sir William Flinders Petrie, and the Egypt Exploration Society. The rules of these societies provide that all objects found go to public museums in proportion to the amount subscribed from various localities. As Dr. Haworth continued to subscribe largely, Manchester has always received a goodly share.

Jesse Haworth, a successful and highly esteemed textile manufacturer, developed a passion for Egyptology, apparently first aroused by reading Amelia B. Edwards' book *A Thousand Miles up the Nile* which described the author's own journey. Some five years later, in 1882, Jesse Haworth and his wife travelled up the Nile and on their return never ceased to pursue their interest in Egyptology. A subsequent meeting with Miss Edwards prompted Jesse Haworth to give financial support to the subject, and in 1887 he began to fund Petrie's excavations in Egypt at Illahun, Kahun and Gurob.

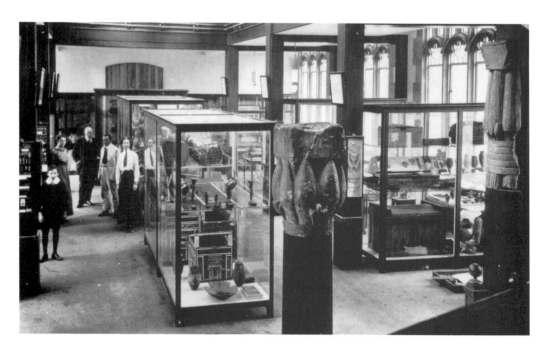

Fig. 26 *The Egyptian Gallery, Manchester Museum in 1912. The generous patronage of Dr Jesse Haworth not only created the Egyptian collection, but also enabled the Museum building to be extended to accommodate this rapidly increasing range of artefacts*

The first major Egyptian acquisition made by the Manchester Museum had been the gift of a mummy with its coffins which had belonged to Asru, a Chantress of Amun in the Temple of Karnak. These were presented to the Manchester Natural History Society (the nucleus of the later museum) in 1825, and it was claimed that 'This was one of the best preserved mummies in the kingdom.' However, it was Jesse Haworth who contributed most to Manchester's Egyptian collection. In 1890 he and Martyn Kennard (the co-sponsor of Petrie's Fayoum excavations) presented a unique and valuable set of objects of daily use, drawn from the Egyptian town sites of Kahun and Gurob. These constituted one of the best collections of Egyptian antiquities in Britain, and were only the first of a succession of gifts which he went on to make to the museum, mainly acquired from Petrie's excavations which, for nine years, were dependent on Haworth's financial support.

Manchester Museum had come into existence in 1821, when the Manchester Society of Natural History was formed to acquire the collections of a Mr J. L. Phillips. The society was disbanded in 1862 because of financial difficulties, and the governors of Manchester's university (then Owens College) took over the collections and the administration of the museum for the benefit of the students and the public. A new building was erected in 1888 to house the museum; it formed an integral part of the main university building, and was designed by the famous architect, Alfred Waterhouse.

By 1911 Jesse Haworth's generous donations of Egyptian antiquities required additional space so that they could be appropriately displayed, and in 1912 Haworth provided two-thirds of the funding required to build an extension which would mainly house the Egyptian collections. This was designed by Alfred Waterhouse's son, Paul. The following year, in recognition of his position as one of the first patrons of scientific excavation, the university conferred on Jesse Haworth the honorary degree of Doctor of Laws. A second museum extension, designed by the third generation of the Waterhouse family, was opened by Jesse Haworth's widow in 1927; this provided further display and storage area for the ever increasing Egyptian collections. Once again, Haworth had been the main benefactor: under the terms of his Will, he made further significant donations, and in addition, his own private collection of Egyptian antiquities came to the museum.

During the years of Jesse Haworth's patronage, Manchester became a major centre for Egyptology. Petrie now held the first chair of Egyptology in Britain, at University College London, and he gave an annual museum lecture in Manchester, providing a progress report on his current excavations. In 1906, his audience listened with rapt attention for an hour and a half, and when he finally appealed for public support for his future excavations, a local society was formed – the Manchester Egyptian Association – with the aim of furthering in every possible way the study of Egyptology in Manchester. Jesse Howarth became the association's first president, with Professor Boyd Dawkins as its vice-president; it attracted important and influential speakers, with Sir William Flinders Petrie and Lady Petrie returning to Manchester to give an annual lecture, and the famous anatomist Professor Grafton Elliot Smith addressing a large audience in 1910 on the subject of his researches on the 'Royal Mummies'.

On 6 May 1908, the association witnessed a significant event in Egyptian palaeopathology. Instead of holding the usual meeting, the members and their friends were invited to attend the unwrapping of one of the 12th Dynasty mummies known as the Two Brothers, which had been received the previous year as part of a complete tomb-group discovered during the excavations by the British School of Archaeology in Egypt, at the site of Der Rifeh in Middle Egypt. Dr Margaret Murray was the director of this research project: as one of Petrie's most able students, she had been seconded by him to Manchester to undertake duties as the museum's first curator of Egyptology. She was the first woman in Britain to hold a full-time appointment in Egyptology, and eventually in 1924 she became assistant professor at University College London.

Her multidisciplinary scientific study of the mummies of the Two Brothers changed existing attitudes towards the examination of mummified remains. The unwrapping took place in the Chemical Theatre of the university, Margaret Murray conducting the proceedings with the assistance of four other members of staff. According to a contemporary report, 'The unrolling was witnessed by five hundred people and lasted one and a half hours. At the close of the ceremony, members of the audience who wished to have a piece of the mummy wrappings as a memento were invited by the Chairman of the meeting to leave their names and addresses.'

In both this original study (Murray, 1910) and the current Manchester project (David, 1979), the human remains of the brothers, named Nekht-Ankh and Khnum-Nakht, have produced some interesting pathological results. Margaret Murray's investigation showed that two very different methods of mummification had been used for the brothers. Nekht-Ankh's viscera were separately preserved and placed in a set of canopic jars; his brother's mummy was less well preserved and he had no accompanying set of jars. Although the coffin inscriptions state that both men had the same mother, named Aa-Khnumu, there is no account of their paternal ancestry. Since the original and current studies both indicate that the men have very different anatomical features, it is possible that they were only half-brothers, with different fathers, or even that one was adopted into the family. Future DNA studies on samples of tissues or bone taken from these bodies may provide an answer to this question.

Radiological examinations of other collections of mummies were carried out over the intervening years, but until 1975 no other mummy was the subject of a multidisciplinary autopsy and investigation in Britain. Then the unwrapping of Mummy 1770 (the person's name was unknown and therefore the museum accession number was used as a form of reference) took place in Manchester. It was a news-worthy event. In front of a specially invited audience that included members of the press and television teams, the procedure began on 10 June 1975, in the Manchester University Medical School. The mummy, wrapped in layers of dull brown bandages, lay on the operating table, the arc lights picking out and highlighting its gilded face mask with its inlaid artificial eyes. Gathered around, in green gowns and masks, were the team members of the Manchester Egyptian Mummy Research Project who brought a range of techniques and skills to this extensive investigation. This was a key event in the Manchester Project which, since 1972, had set out to examine the collection of human and animal mummified remains in the Manchester Museum.

The multidisciplinary team was drawn from the university and elsewhere and had two aims: to discover more information about living conditions, disease, and causes of death in the ancient Egyptian population; and to establish a methodology for examining mummified remains which other institutions could adapt to study their own collections. From 1973 to 1975, the Manchester mummies (then numbering seventeen human – to which another five have since been added – and thirty-four animal) were investigated, using a range of techniques which included radiology, histopathology and electron microscopy, dental examination, scientific facial reconstruction, and finger-printing. It was decided to include the autopsy in 1975, because the team considered that investigative techniques had advanced sufficiently to ensure that much new information would be gained from such a total procedure. In the case of Mummy 1770, not only did they employ the techniques already used for the other mummies, but there was also the opportunity to carry out Carbon-14 dating on the bones and bandages, and to describe the nature of the bandage textiles, identifying them microscopically and macroscopically, as well as using chromatographic and other techniques to isolate and characterize the substances that had been applied to the bandages. This first phase of the project also included experimental studies in mummification to assess the accuracy of the Classical writers, and the use of electron microscopy to identify insects found in association with the mummies.

By 1979 this first phase was completed and was marked in several ways: a scientific account of the work gave details of the

Fig. 27 *In 1975 the Manchester Mummy Team decided to unwrap and investigate Mummy 1770, the first time such a total examination had been undertaken in Britain since 1908. Here, the first cuts are made in the bandages of the mummy, which belonged to a 14-year-old girl whose legs had been amputated shortly before death*

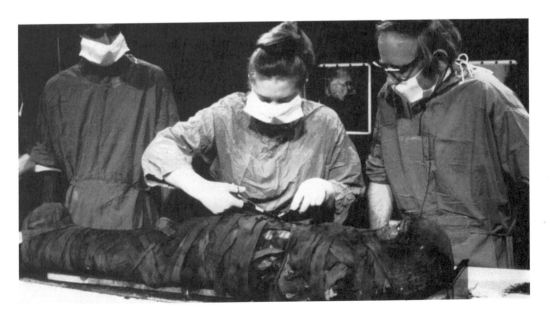

aims, techniques and results (David, 1979), and a more general book outlined the range of techniques used by the team and related the story of Mummy 1770 (David, 1978). In Manchester, the first international symposium entitled 'Science in Egyptology' was held, at which scholars and scientists from many countries met to discuss the application of scientific techniques in the field of mummified remains. The British Broadcasting Corporation produced a television film in their 'Chronicle' series which covered the work of the project and, in particular, the unwrapping of Mummy 1770, and two short films were also made by the university's audio-visual service. The longer of these showed the various methods and techniques used to examine the Manchester mummies, and was given the major film award of the British Association for the Advancement of Science for 'the most effective presentation to a non-specialist audience of a scientific or technological subject'. The other film, which recorded the main events in the investigation of Mummy 1770, won one of the five certificates of merit presented by the same organization. In 1979–80, the team's work was also presented in a public exhibition at the Manchester Museum; entitled 'O, Osiris, Live Forever!', it featured the scientific investigation and results against the general background of Egyptian religious beliefs and customs. It attracted many visitors, and received the Sotheby's Award for the best temporary exhibition in Britain in the Museum of the Year competition for 1980. Later, selected material from this display toured the country and also travelled to Canada, where it formed the nucleus of an exhibition held in Edmonton as one of the celebrations held to mark the seventy-fifth anniversary of the University of Alberta.

After 1979, the team decided to expand the range of techniques further. Major diagnostic tools such as radiology and histopathology were continued and developed, and serological studies were added. Most important, however, was the introduction of endoscopy as a means of obtaining tissue for histology without the need to unwrap or dissect the mummies (see Chapter 11). Indeed, Manchester has continued to promote the idea of using virtually non-destructive techniques, and recently, new advances have been made which enable the scientific reconstruction of heads to be undertaken, without it first being necessary to unwrap the mummy (see Chapter 13).

At the 1979 symposium in Manchester, the idea was first proposed and accepted that an International Mummy Database should be established at the Manchester Museum, designed first to gather and store information about disease discovered in Egyptian mummies, and then to supply data to researchers on the occurrence and possibly the patterns of disease which might

Fig. 28 (opposite) *The mummy of a young man, dating from the first century BC. The elaborate diagonal bandaging is interspersed with gild studs; both features are typical of this later period. This portrait is finely painted, providing a likeness of the individual owner, but X-rays have revealed that the mummy is a jumble of bones within the wrappings*

Fig. 29 *The mummy of a child examined by the Manchester team. The face (with faint traces of gilding) has the dark, resinous appearance typical of mummies of the Graeco-Roman period. Relatively few mummies of children before the Graeco-Roman period have been found, perhaps indicating that elaborate funerary rites were usually reserved for adults*

emerge at different periods of Egypt's history. An ongoing project, this database will ultimately be of use to specialists in a number of disciplines.

Other results from the work carried out since 1979 have included another book which concentrates on the non-destructive approach and on the new techniques that the team have introduced in recent years (David and Tapp, 1984), and a second BBC television film in the 'Chronicle' series, filmed in Egypt and in Manchester, which looked at aspects of life and death in ancient Egypt. Another film, made by the Central Office of Information for distribution abroad, was entitled 'Blessings of the Mummies', and this related how techniques developed in the Mummy Research Project had benefited the modern world. The fingerprinting method, specially devised for use on the Manchester mummies, has subsequently been introduced into the standard practices of some police forces, and knowledge obtained from the scientific reconstruction of three-dimensional heads of some of the mummies has been of benefit in the field of plastic surgery.

In 1984, Manchester University played host to the second international meeting 'Science in Egyptology', and the Proceedings of both these symposia were later published (David, 1986). To coincide with the 1984 symposium, the first phase of the redisplayed permanent Egyptian galleries at the Manchester Museum was opened; this exhibit features the funerary beliefs and customs of the Egyptians, and the research and results of the team's work. Later, the second gallery was opened; this concentrated on aspects of daily life and technology in ancient Egypt. Both these displays were ultimately judged for the Museum of the Year Award which Manchester won in 1987.

Egyptian mummies are a valuable source of information; they not only contribute to our understanding of funerary beliefs and social customs, but they also provide a unique opportunity to detect traces of disease in ancient populations. However, they are also a finite resource, vulnerable to deterioration because of a range of conditions, and every attempt should be made to rectify any existing damage and to protect them against further problems. In research studies, Egyptologists, palaeopathologists and conservators need to work together to ensure that maximum information is gained while making minimal use of intrusive or destructive techiques.

The next phase of the Manchester Project will seek to build on the results of the last twenty years, expanding and developing the techniques which have proved to be useful and successful in the past. An exciting possibility is offered by the new methods associated with DNA studies, only now made available through recent advances in this field.

8

The Radiological Investigation

Ian Isherwood and C. W. Hart

From the earliest days following the discovery of x-rays by Röntgen in 1895 there has been considerable interest in the value of radiology in the investigation of mummified Egyptian remains. The first radiographs of mummified material (a child and a cat) were obtained by a German investigator, König, in Frankfurt in March 1896. A month later in Liverpool the English x-ray pioneer Thurstan Holland illustrated a mummified bird. He commented at the time that the 'advantage of this class of subject is that there is no movement'. At that time x-ray exposures were many minutes, compared with milliseconds using modern radiological equipment. In 1898 Sir Flinders Petrie made use of x-rays in the investigation of human mummified remains, and shortly afterwards in 1904 Elliot Smith, assisted by Howard Carter, x-rayed the mummy of Tuthmosis IV. They later told of their experience in transferring the rigid pharaoh by taxicab to a private x-ray unit in Cairo. The condition of the growing ends of the king's long bones, the epiphyses, enabled his age at the time of death to be estimated with precision.

A number of important radiological surveys have been carried out by several workers over the years. Such scientific surveys were pioneered in particular by Moodie in 1931 in the United States and by the British radiologist Dr P.H.K. Gray, who documented important collections in Leiden in 1966, in the City of Liverpool Museum in 1968 and, with W.R. Dawson, the Egyptian mummies of the British Museum, also in 1968.

Detailed radiological studies have contributed significantly to the identification of historical Egyptian figures and some of the techniques employed are now well established in forensic practice.

Until recent years most recorded specimens were radiographed on site, either in museums or at archaeological sites. In these circumstances the investigation is significantly limited by the need to use mobile equipment with limited power. Important advances in x-ray apparatus, methods of image display and of course in medical radiodiagnosis itself have been made in the hundred or so years since Röntgen's discovery, and it is now inconceivable to think of a hospital in a developed country without a Department of Clinical Radiology. The basic principles of x-ray production and transmission have not changed, but considerable sophistication has been added to the manner in which areas of special interest may be explored and the facilities with which the image may be viewed. Modern x-ray techniques include fluoroscopy, orbiting manoeuvres, and tomography as routine, with computed tomography (CT) available in an increasing number of hospitals and medical schools.

Fluoroscopy, that is, the visualization of transmitted x-rays on a television screen, provides an immediate and dynamic view of events to the observer. The three-dimensional nature of an object is readily perceived by moving it in the x-ray beam whilst visualization of moving parts in a living patient by this method is routine practice. Video recordings of the television image are readily available. The development of specialized radiological equipment capable of orbiting around the subject enables the observer to view the x-ray image by television link from any angle without moving the subject at all. Tomography is a method of obtaining x-rays of a section or slice of tissue in a plane of interest, rather like taking one card from a pack of cards. This is achieved in conventional tomography by blurring out the unwanted shadows above and below the plane of interest, the image of which is then left more sharply defined. Computed tomography is an x-ray transmission technique developed in Britain by Sir Godfrey Hounsfield in the early 1970s. The x-ray beam is highly collimated and the radiographic film replaced by sensitive detectors. Such a system enables thin cross sections of a patient or object to be calculated from precise measurements of transmitted x-radiation. Sections can be as thin as 1–2 mm. The transmission data are processed by computer and made available either as digital information or, by analog conversion, as a pictorial display on a television monitor. Computed tomography not only eliminates the problem of superimposition completely but also, with powerful image-processing techniques and interactive displays, provides the opportunity for an observer to interrogate in detail the contents of the image. The method is very sensitive and provides information which may not be visualized by plain radiography or conventional tomography. Since each transverse section consists of a fine matrix of digital information, a number of contiguous thin sections can be thought of as a block of digital data. Such a block can be 'cut' in different directions using computer technology, thus providing the possibility for creating images in alternative planes. This process is referred to as 'reformatting'. By introducing a further dimension of distance from the observer a truly three-dimensional image can be produced; this can be rotated in any direction on the television monitor and can also be processed to emphasize soft tissue or bony detail.

The radiological investigation of mummified remains can be difficult because of the heavy and dense casing in which such mummified specimens are housed, combined with the problem of artefacts of varying density in complex wrappings. There are obvious advantages in being able to conduct the radiological investigation of archaeological remains in specialized radiological departments; it is then possible to 'look inside' the object in order to select the best radiological projections, and to carry out specialized techniques such as computed tomography. Another important advantage is that controlled and rapid (e.g 90 seconds) film-processing facilities are immediately available.

There are two main areas of interest in the x-ray investigation of human remains – one concerned with the archaeology of the specimen and its relationship to the timescale of cultural development, and the other with the scientific study of disease, injury and causes of death in ancient civilizations. The term palaeopathology was devised by Ruffer in 1913 for the latter group.

Archaeology

The first requirement is to identify the presence or absence of human or animal tissue. When the mummified remains are clearly exposed this does not present a problem, but elaborate bandaging and outer coverings can be deceptive, particularly in animal mummies. A number of 'forgeries' or puzzling artefacts have been noted by most observers.

The evaluation of Egyptological collections in museums presents difficulties since the material is usually drawn from a very extended timescale. Comment on individual specimens is therefore inevitably anecdotal and dependent upon comparison with data from other studies. Seventeen complete human mummies investigated and recorded in detail from the Manchester Museum (Isherwood et al, 1978 and 1979, and Fawcitt et al,

1984) covered a timescale from 1900 BC to the fourth century AD and an equally wide geographical distribution from Hawara to Thebes.

The particular features of archaeological interest in the study of human mummies include the age and sex of the individual, the embalming techniques employed, the presence or absence of disease and ante-mortem injury. X-ray examination presents a unique opportunity to evaluate skeletal maturity and development. The formation of bone begins in the foetus at certain main centres during pregnancy and progresses at some sites well into adult life. The timescale for bony development varies in different parts of the body. Over a hundred such ossification centres, i.e. sites of bone development, can be studied in the skeletal assessment of age in human beings. The six most important body sites are the hands, feet, elbows, knees, shoulders and hips. There are modern well-documented European and North American radiological standards to define bone age with accuracy. It is important to appreciate, however, when considering the bone age of an ancient Egyptian mummy that there may be significant racial differences as a consequence of genetic and nutritional factors. To be truly accurate radiological standards should not only be of the same ethnic group but also of a contemporary population.

In a number of mummies the genitalia can be identified to enable the sex of the individual to be determined easily. Where doubt exists it is necessary to consider specific skeletal features relating to the size and shape of particular bones, especially the pelvis. There are however significant variations and overlaps between the sexes.

The process of mummification developed over the centuries from predynastic dessication in hot sand to elaborate stylized ceremonial in the later dynasties, reaching a peak at the 21st Dynasty with subsequent decline towards the Roman Period. Detailed radiological investigation has enabled considerable information to be gained about the techniques employed by those responsible for the embalming. The posture of the subject, and particularly the position of the arms and hands, may be significant, together with the general disposition and organization of the remains. The arms may be extended and hands at the sides resting on the thighs or over the pubic region. When the arms are crossed over the chest the left hand may be clenched, suggesting the Osiris position. The position of the arms and hands on radiographs of 111 mummies were reviewed and evaluated by Gray in 1972. A similar study was carried out in the Manchester mummies in 1978. Most mummies from the 21st to the 25th Dynasties have extended arms.

The essential process of mummification consisted of dehydration and dessication. The abdominal organs and lungs were usually removed by an incision into the left flank. Before the 21st Dynasty the viscera were placed in canopic jars, but in later periods were returned to the body cavity in four or more separate packs. The body and viscera up to the 25th Dynasty were treated with natron, a mixture of sodium bicarbonate and sodium carbonate, as a dehydrating agent. Later, more reliance was placed on the use of resin applied in the molten state when, in the words of W. R. Dawson, it might 'invade every crevice of the cavity and even the cancellous structure of bone'. In Roman times natron was often used again. Body cavity packing materials varied from sawdust to linen and mud. The soft tissues of the face, trunk and limbs from the 21st to the 26th Dynasty were on occasion restored by subcutaneous packing via small incisions.

To remove the brain during embalming special instrumentation described by Herodotus was carried out through the nostrils to avoid disfigurement. This inevitably resulted in damage to the thin plate of bone separating the nasal cavity from the interior of the skull. In the Manchester Museum study recorded in 1978 the presence of such characteristic bone defects was detected in mummies ranging from the 12th Dynasty to the Roman Period.

Whilst the Egyptians made no formal attempt to preserve the eye globe some form of resoration, using mud or linen or even artificial eyes, was employed for cosmetic reasons. The eye globe was allowed to recede to the back of the orbit during mummification. Shrunken eyeballs, ocular muscles and the optic nerve have been identified by direct investigation. In the present study computed tomography was employed for this purpose.

Amulets of religious significance were often placed in the wrappings and, being made of ceramic or metal, sometimes gold, are easily detected radiologically. A rectangular plate has on occasions been demonstrated overlying the left flank incision.

Palaeopathology

Radiology provides important insights into the presence or absence of disease. Evidence of trauma can sometimes be found and conjecture made about the possible cause of death.

Bones and joints, subject to the normal wear and tear of everyday living, frequently exhibit evidence of degeneration. Such change is shown by the development of bony spurs and thickening from those joints under stress. The joints themselves may become narrowed, findings which are most frequently observed in the spine, the hips and the hands. The

Fig. 30 *Natsef-Amun's mummy was first examined by Miss C.W. Hart using conventional radiography*

distribution and frequency of such changes do not appear to differ from ancient Egypt to the present day. Intervertebral disc spaces are often narrowed in older individuals due to degeneration of the disc material. Secondary changes in the adjacent vertebrae then occur. Fractures and dislocations have been detected in some mummies, but very often these are the result of damage after death.

A variety of disease processes have been discovered in the radiological investigations of previous research workers, but there has been a notable absence of certain 'modern' diseases such as cancer, syphilis, tuberculosis and rickets. Stones in the gall bladder and kidneys have been reported, together with calcification in blood vessels indicating arteriosclerosis.

Radiology of the Leeds Mummy, Natsef-Amun

The radiological investigations on Natsef-Amun were all carried out in the Department of Diagnostic Radiology in the Medical School, University of Manchester. It was necessary to handle the mummified remains with particular care because of their exposed condition and also because of an unstable transverse fracture through the lower lumbar spine.

Conventional radiological studies were first undertaken commencing with the head and proceeding to the feet (Fig. 30). The hands, which were detached, were examined separately. It was not necessary to carry out fluoroscopy, since most structures were directly visible. Radiographic projections appropriate to

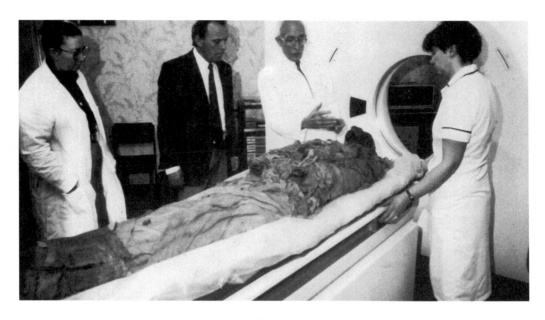

Fig. 31 *Natsef-Amun entering the CT scanner*

modern clinical investigations were carried out using a conventional x-ray tube. Kodak X-Omatic film with calcium tungstate screens were used throughout. Test exposures were first obtained to optimize the radiographic factors, i.e. kilovoltages, milliamps and time of exposure.

On completion of the conventional studies the mummy was transferred to the CT scanner in an adjacent room. Here the whole body was subjected to a transaxial sectional survey (Fig. 31).

Plain Films

The most striking feature about the skull was the removal of the posterior part of the skull vault. The character of the cut edges of the defect suggested that this bone removal was of recent origin (Fig. 32). Packing was noted in the nasal cavity and in the oropharynx (Fig. 33). The pituitary fossa was normal and the frontal sinuses well developed. All the remaining teeth showed evidence of excessive attrition, i.e. increased wear on the biting surface of the teeth. This feature, characteristic of many ancient Egyptian teeth, has been well described and is almost certainly due to the coarse and unrefined diet of those days, particularly the bread (see Chapter 9).

The cervical spine showed evidence of intervertebral disc space narrowing between the 5th and 6th cervical segments. There were associated osteophytes, i.e. bony protrusions, both in front of and behind the abnormal disc. The appearances are typical of a degenerative cervical disc which would almost cer-

*Radiographs of
Natsef-Amun's skull*

Fig. 32 (above)*This lateral
view clearly shows the
sharply defined hole in the
back of the skull, and the
attrition of the cusps of the
teeth*

Fig. 33 (below) *The
packing in the nasal
airways can be seen in this
antero-posterior view of the
skull*

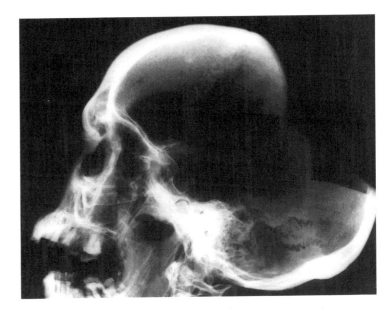

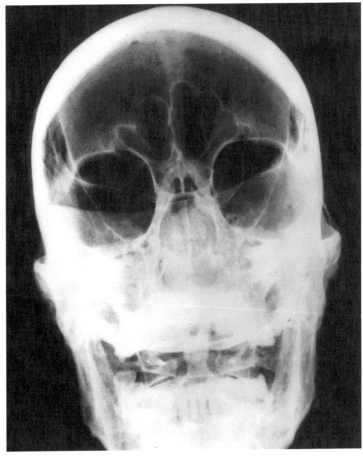

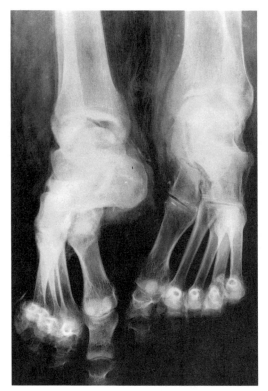

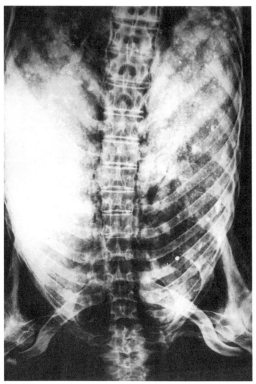

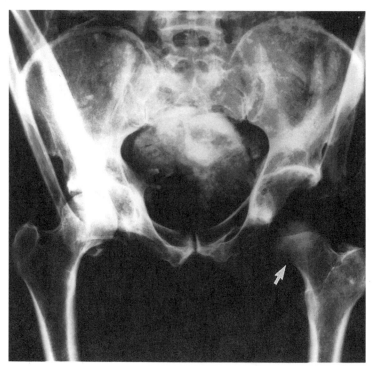

Radiographs of Natsef-Amun's mummy showing:

Fig. 34 (above left) *the feet. The deformity which can be seen is probably due to tight bandaging rather than any congenital abnormality*

Fig. 35 (above right) *the thorax. Packing can be seen on both sides of the thorax*

Fig. 36 (right) *the pelvis. Packing can be seen in the pelvic cavity. Changes in the left femoral head caused by osteoarthritis are indicated by the arrow*

tainly have been responsible for intermittent pain in the neck, possibly radiating into the arms. The appearances are identical to those seen in many middle to older age group individuals of the present day. The thoracic spine appeared entirely normal, whilst the lumbar spine was disarticulated at the level of the 4th and 5th lumbar intervertebral disc. This disarticulation is a post-mortem artefact and almost certainly of recent origin. There was no evidence of degenerative disc disease in the lumbar spine. In particular, no evidence of calcific deposits could be detected in the intervertebral discs. Calcification has been observed in the intervertebral disc spaces of an unusual number of Egyptian mummies. Whilst attempts have been made in the past to attribute this finding to a rare inborn metabolic disorder known as alkaptonuria, it is considered by most authors (Gray, 1967) to be the effect of the embalming procedure. A study of these changes, including biopsy and spectroscopy, was carried out in the Manchester mummy series (Isherwood et al., 1979) confirming that such changes could not have occurred in life.

The arms of Natsef-Amun were extended and although the hands had been detached the disposition of the limbs suggests that the hands would originally have been over the inner surfaces of the thighs. This is a typical position observed in other mummies from the 21st Dynasty both by Gray in 1972 and in the Manchester mummies described in 1978. No abnormalities could be detected in the arms or hands, though the outlines of the finger nails can be clearly discerned.

In the lower limbs the feet were deformed but there was no evidence of arthritis or secondary bone changes in the feet, which might have suggested a long-standing congenital abnormality (Fig. 34). Similar deformities have been observed in other mummies including Khnum-Nakht, one of two brothers in the Manchester Mummy Collection, and the matter has been debated by several authorities in the past, including Murray in 1910 and Isherwood et al. in 1979. The Khnum-Nakht foot and the present study supports the theory that the findings are due to excessively tight wrapping after death rather than to any congenital anomaly.

The thoracic cavity was packed with material of heterogeneous and varying density (Fig. 35). There was no evidence of the heart or lungs remaining, though these have been described in other mummies. No specific packages could be identified. In the abdomen and pelvis similar packing material was noted and examined in more detail by computed tomography.

The left hip joint was disarticulated, due to post-mortem damage. Small subcortical cysts were, however, observed in the head of the femur on the left side (Fig. 36). These appearances are associated with early osteoarthritis of the hip.

Computed tomography

Computed tomography was carried out from the head to the feet in thin tranaxial slices. In the skull a digital scannergram was first carried out to enable the transaxial sections to be accurately located. 3 mm contiguous sections were obtained in the skull from 70.5 mm above the external auditory canal, i.e. the outer orifice of the ear, to 76.5 mm below it. Fifty of these 3 mm sections were obtained, enabling computer reformatting in alternative planes to be carried out. Three-dimensional images of both soft tissue and bone were then obtained in a variety of rotations (Figs. 37 and 38).

A notable feature of the thin transaxial sections through the orbits was the revelation of the optic nerve and ocular muscles behind the collapsed globe of the eye. By computer techniques alternative sections were constructed through and across the optic nerve and ocular muscles demonstrating their true position within the orbital cavity. Whilst the presence of the optic nerve and ocular muscles have been observed in other mummies by direct dissection (Sandison, 1967 and 1986) this is believed to be the first time that these structures have been demonstrated non-invasively using computed tomography.

The optic nerves have of course been severed behind the orbits during the removal of the brain. The route of removal of the brain through the thin ethmoidal plates separating the nasal cavity from the anterior cranial fossa can be clearly seen. Packing is present in the nasopharynx, the oropharynx and the oral cavity. Packing material extends to the outer aspect of the upper teeth, padding out the upper cheeks (Fig. 39).

Details of the middle and inner ear can be seen using the very thin computer sections processed with an appropriate bone algorithm. The detailed anatomy of the inner ear, including the semicircular canals, the auditory ossicles and the cochlea, can all be identified.

In the spine resinous material can be identified within the spinal canal normally occupied by the spinal cord and nerves. A ring-like density in the cervical spinal canal suggests that the dura – the membranous lining of the canal – is still present. An increased density can also be seen in the vertebral artery canal of the cervical spine, suggesting that the remains of the vertebral arteries might still be present.

In the thorax two layers of packing can be identified. The first is very dense and crescentic, more on the left than the right, and situated at the back of the thorax with a little immediately in front of the vertebral bodies. This is presumably resin introduced after the removal of the heart and lungs. In front of this crescentic and fixed resinous material is a much less dense

Three dimensional computed tomography depicting (Fig. 37, above) *the soft tissues of the face and* (Fig. 38, below) *the bony detail of the face*

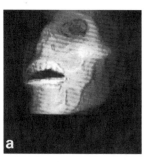

a

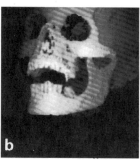

b

Fig. 39 *Transverse CT section through the skull, showing the packing present in both cheeks*

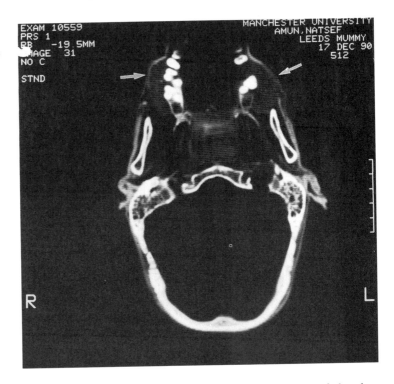

heterogeneous packing material filling the remains of the thoracic cavity. This latter packing appears more recent than the resinous material, which is fixed in the thoracic cavity. The soft tissue density in the centre of the thoracic cavity could represent the remains of the heart and mediastium, which have been clearly identified in several of the Manchester mummies. In the abdomen similar appearances were obtained with a particular preponderance of the recent heterogeneous packing. There was no evidence of individual organ packs. No abnormality was seen in the sacroiliac joints or joints of the spine.

In summary, there are many artefacts detected in the radiological investigation of Natsef-Amun due to the previous unwrapping and later damage. Nevertheless, several interesting features have been detected, notably the presence of the optic nerves and ocular muscles. The evidence of brain removal, the position of the arms, the presence of resinous material in the thoracic and abdominal cavities, together with packing material in the nasopharynx and oropharynx suggest a particular attention to embalming technique typical of the 21st Dynasty. The absence of any particular disease process except for degenerative arthritis in the neck and possibly the hip is not surprising. It is rare to be able to detect the cause of death with certainty in ancient Egyptian mummies.

9 The Dental Examination of Natsef-Amun

Judith Miller and Catherine Asher-McDade

Teeth become brittle through the passage of time but they are virtually indestructible and a thorough dental examination of the mummy is the key to much information about the health and diet of Natsef-Amun in his lifetime.

The ancient Egyptian is considered to have had a very healthy diet by present-day standards. Evidence for this can be found in tomb reliefs and paintings and on funerary stelae which show foods considered necessary to sustain the mummy in the after-life, and include products enjoyed in the lifetime of the mummy. Bread and beer were of great importance in the diet and a typical lunch for an Egyptian workman consisted of bread, beer and onions (Fig. 40). The banks of the Nile were very fertile. Barley and wheat, used for flour-making, were grown as well as various pulses such as chick peas and lentils. Vegetables included lettuces, marrows, courgettes, cucumbers, garlic and onions. Melons, figs, dates, grapes and pomegranates were plentiful and wine was made from grapes and pomegranates. Beef was a luxury but mutton, goat and pork were eaten. Fish were caught in the river and dried, salted or pickled. The nobility hunted wildfowl, and ducks and geese were kept in pens and their eggs were eaten.

As Natsef-Amun was a priest he would have lived and worked in the temple for three months of the year. As part of his duties

Fig. 40 *Scene on a block from the Aten Temple, Karnak, showing a workman eating his lunch. The basket contains bread, cucumber and onion*

he would have performed the daily temple ritual in which he presented morning, midday and evening meals to the god in the sanctuary. After completion of these rituals the food was given to the priest as payment. This food would have been the finest available. During the rest of the year the priest would continue to eat well as he came from a privileged level of society.

It is difficult to believe that this diet could be the cause of dental problems but bread was the culprit. It was the most important food in the diet, to the extent that the ancient Egyptians were called *artophagoi* which means 'eaters of bread'. Bread was placed in their tombs for the afterlife and, because of the dry, airless atmosphere in the tombs, some of this bread has been preserved in excellent condition. Samples can be found in many Egyptology collections in museums worldwide, and thirteen specimens were examined in a study by F. F. Leek (1972). Three were from the Manchester Museum and were from Sedment, 6th Dynasty; Deir el Bahari, 9th Dynasty; and Gurob 18th Dynasty. Others came from collections in Oxford, Scotland, Holland, France, Italy and the USA. The majority of these specimens originated in Thebes. Microscopic examination of the bread revealed the presence of husks of corn and mineral particles, and radiological examination clearly showed inorganic material. These particles were isolated chemically and photographed, enlarged × 105. The samples were also analyzed petrographically and were found to contain mainly quartz grains but there was also feldspar, mica and hornblende. The quartz grains were rounded and were probably sand.

The inorganic material would have been introduced at several stages in the manufacture of the bread. The grain was initially crushed in a limestone mortar and then ground in a saddle quern (Fig. 41). Apart from contamination from the stone of the

Fig. 41 *Figure of a woman grinding corn. The flour would be contaminated by stone from the mortar and quern and by windblown sand, but a percentage of sand was also probably deliberately added to the grain to facilitate the grinding process*

Fig. 42 *Two bakers work in the kitchen of Ramesses III. The cylindrical oven has an open top from which flames burst forth; the round loaves, carried by one man on a tray, were cooked on the outside of the oven. (After Rosselini)*

mortar and quern, the wind-blown desert sand would be incorporated in the flour. In experiments carried out by A. J. N. W. Prag of Manchester Museum it was discovered that corn ground in saddlestones for fifteen minutes showed little change unless a percentage of sand was added; this resulted in the production of fine flour. Pliny wrote that the Carthaginians used this technique and it is likely that the Egyptians also deliberately added some sand to the grain. The flour was sieved but the sieve was too coarse to remove all the impurities or the husks of the partially crushed grains (Fig. 43). The flat loaves were then baked on a stone on a fire or directly on the outside walls of the oven and in this way even more contaminants were introduced (Fig. 42).

Coarse bread was not just a problem for the poor; even the pharaohs suffered from its harsh consequences. In the story of Joseph, in Genesis, the baker is imprisoned and then beheaded, and Polano, in *Selections from the Talmud*, has suggested that this was because Pharaoh was angry about the gritty bread.

In modern man there are two main dental problems, tooth decay and diseases of the gums and supporting tissues. Decay or dental caries is endemic. It is caused by the action of bacteria on refined sugars in the diet contained in the plaque lying on the surface of the tooth. However, refined sugars were unknown in Egypt until the time of the Ptolemies in 332 BC, and food was sweetened with honey and fruits such as dates; consequently dental decay was only a minor problem. Nevertheless, the ancient Egyptian suffered from severe dental disease.

The bulk or core of the human tooth is made of dentine, a highly mineralized material which is well preserved in mummies. It is identical in formation to ivory. A layer of enamel coats the crown of the tooth and a layer of cement, similar in structure to dentine, coats the root of the tooth. Enamel is the hardest, most highly mineralized substance in the body and is as hard as sapphire. The teeth are thus frequently the best preserved parts of the mummies.

Unfortunately, the diet described above had harmful effects on the ancient Egyptians' teeth. The impurities in their bread and other foods caused the teeth to be worn down. The occlusal or grinding surface of the molars and pre molars would begin to show signs of damage even during childhood. The pointed cusps of the teeth gradually became worn and flattened (attrition) so that the biting surfaces of the back teeth no longer slotted together in one position. Thus, the grinding movement of the lower jaw (mandible) on the upper jaw (maxilla) became wider and less controlled, since it was no longer limited by the relationship of the cusps of the opposing teeth. This damaged the jaw joint (temporo mandibular joint) and the jaw bone (alveolar bone) which supported the teeth. The teeth could therefore become loosened. This tooth wear continued throughout life.

Once the dentine layers beneath the enamel are exposed, the teeth become sensitive to changes in temperature. As a reaction to the attrition of the enamel and dentine, there is a protective mechanism whereby extra (secondary) dentine is laid down inside the nerve (pulp) of the tooth. This thickens the dentine layers and protects the exquisitely sensitive pulp. In many cases, the tooth wear was so rapid in ancient Egyptians that the secondary dentine was not laid down sufficiently quickly and the result was that the pulp became exposed. The consequence of this was severe pain and the introduction of bacteria into the previously protected pulp. This infection could then travel down the root canal and penetrate the surrounding supporting bone at the base of the tooth; the result was the formation of an abscess around the apex of the root. Abscesses could also form in the supporting tissues in association with the breakdown of the bone and the loosening of the teeth. In severe cases, when the infection was unable to drain out of the jaw, osteomyelitis (sepsis of the bone) and septicaemia (sepsis of the blood) would occur. A study of the skull of Ramesses II shows evidence that he died from this condition and must have suffered years of severe pain at the end of his life.

The back of Natsef-Amun's skull was sliced off during the original examination of the mummy in 1828. Apart from this, the head and neck are almost complete and the examination of these, including his teeth, has proved invaluable in assessing many facts about Natsef-Amun's life.

He has a normal skull vault but there is evidence of damage to the cranial base of the skull; this is almost certainly post-mortem damage which occurred when the preparation of the body for mummification was being carried out. The pituitary fossa is

Fig. 43 *A sieve used during the processing of flour. Such sieves were too coarse to remove all the impurities of the partially crushed grains*

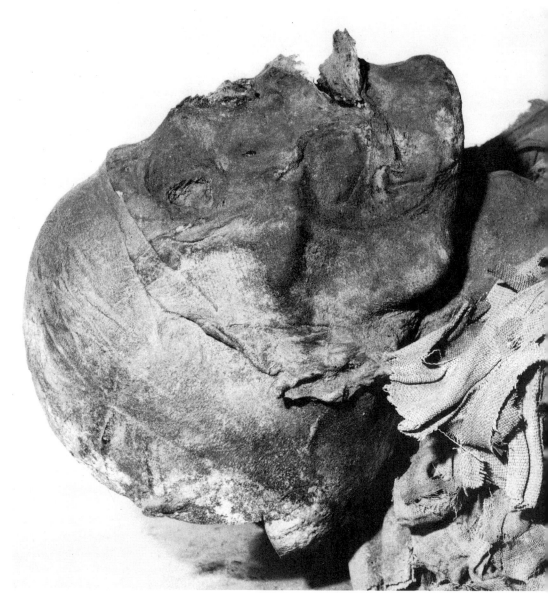

Fig. 44 *The open mouth and protruding tongue seen in the mummy of Natsef-Amun. This is very unusual, and may have been caused by manual strangulation or, more likely, by inflammation of the tongue due to an insect bite*

shallow and long. There is extensive loss of the upper part of the nasal septum, the ethmoids and the conchae – these are the small bones which make up the inside of the nose and which are damaged when the brain tissue is removed during the embalming process.

There is controversy as to the manner of Natsef-Amun's death. He is almost unique in having been mummified with his mouth wide open and his tongue protruding (Fig. 44). It is unusual for the mouth to be open, let alone for the tongue to be

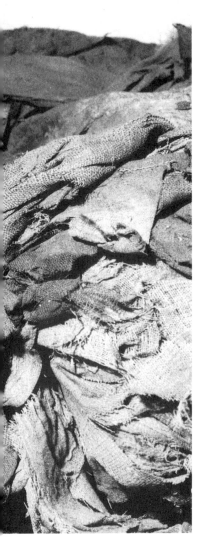

protruding. It would appear from examination of many other mummies that if a person died with his/her mouth open, the embalmers took trouble to apply linen head bandages *post mortem* in order to close the mouth. It is not understood why no attempt was made to close Natsef-Amun's mouth. Did he suffer a violent death? It was certainly not uncommon for priests of his high standing, who were always involved in the political life of Egypt, to meet with unpleasant and violent deaths. One of the theories which has been considered is that Natsef-Amun was strangled. However, the delicate hyoid bone in his neck is intact and it would be difficult to strangle somebody without damage to this small bone at the front of the larynx.

People may die from natural causes with their mouths open and their tongues protruding – following seizures or heart attacks, for example – but, if this was the case, it is strange that no attempt was made to place the tongue inside the mouth and to close the mouth even partially following his death.

The ritual opening of the mouth is a well-documented symbolic ritual which was carried out as part of the preparation of the deceased person for the afterlife. The majority of the evidence suggests that this was a purely symbolic rite which was carried out either on the statue of the person or on the bandaged mummy. If this is so, no actual ceremony would have been performed on the unbandaged corpse. However, a form of ritual may have been carried out on the body itself prior to mummification (Pahl, 1986). The lips of mummified corpses are often found to be in odd positions as if tampering of the lip tissue had occurred *post mortem*. Mummies have been found with wide open mouths and also with almost closed dental arches with the tongue between the front teeth, but only one other mummy has been found with its mouth wide open and the tongue protruding as in this case. This gave us the rare opportunity to study his teeth in detail in addition to making a radiological examination.

Natsef-Amun had all his anterior teeth, i.e. all his incisors, canines and pre molars (Fig. 7). He had lost several molars (back teeth) and this almost certainly occurred during his lifetime as a result of the chronic periodontal disease from which he suffered. His anterior teeth are badly worn, both on their biting surfaces and also interstitially (i.e. on the sides of the teeth). This is almost certainly a combination of attrition and erosion. Attrition occurred as a result of the wear of the teeth due to the diet. He has marked attrition which affects his entire dentition (i.e the number, kind and arrangement of teeth) and is responsible for producing completely flat, cuspless back teeth. The anterior teeth are worn to almost half the normal crown height, all the enamel being worn away and the dentine being exposed. The pattern of this attrition, which was virtually universal during

Natsef-Amun's time, differed between individuals as a result of their ages, the variation in their power to chew, and also in the choice of more or less abrasive foods. In some instances impurities in the diet actually caused the surfaces of teeth to be polished rather than abraded.

It is a little more difficult to explain why the crowns of Natsef-Amun's teeth are so severely worn interstitially but it could have been caused either by chemical attack or by tooth cleaning processes. His anterior teeth look more like small pegs than normally shaped teeth. He may have eaten a large amount of acidic fruit which would have eroded the teeth in this fashion and he may have consumed a high volume of acidic fruit drinks. Alternatively, he may have had a method of dental hygiene which involved polishing the side surfaces of the teeth. There is certainly evidence that, in common with many communities in the third world today, ancient Egyptians used a method of cleaning the teeth with small splayed fragments of twigs. This could have eventually caused wear such as that seen in this case.

One cannot rule out the possibility of accidental damage to his teeth through direct injury to his mouth, for example, in a fall. Certainly the damage to the upper right canine could have been traumatic if it occurred in his lifetime.

In common with the majority of his peers, Natsef-Amun did not have any decay (caries) in his mouth. This reflects the relatively sugar-free diet which he probably enjoyed and the lack of sticky plaque-retaining dietary components.

Following the visual examination of the mummy's teeth, a radiological examination was made. Early one spring morning, Natsef-Amun was brought on a stretcher from his temporary resting place in the Manchester Museum to the University Dental Hospital, luckily only about a hundred metres from the museum. In the Department of Radiography he was gently laid on the examination couch, where radiographs of his head, teeth and neck could be taken under optimal hospital conditions.

The radiographs were taken by Mrs Rush Ashington, Superintendent Radiographer, who has a remarkable ability to radiograph Egyptian mummies, not always the most co-operative of patients . . . She has ingenious ways of radiographing the parts of the mouth which other radiographers cannot reach! The radiographing of Natsef-Amun was no exception in that he required inventive devices in order to produce this set of radiographs. Standard dental and cephalometric x-ray films were used but the exposure times had to be varied to compensate for the odd angles at which it was necessary to take some of the films. In addition, the times for development of the films were varied in order to give clearer images where necessary.

Most mummies are bandaged with their mouths closed and their teeth hidden, so that in the past it has been necessary to take tomograph films of the teeth. Tomography enables the teeth to be isolated from their background and represented relatively sharply against the blurred layers lying above and beneath them. It is particularly useful in the examination of wrapped mummies where the mouth is closed and the teeth would otherwise be obscured. However, in the case of Natsef-Amun, direct intraoral radiographs were taken of individual sections of the mouth, as in a living patient. This was only possible because his mouth was wide open. Small x-ray films, approximately 2×3 cm, were placed directly behind the teeth and the x-ray cone placed so as to obtain a direct view of the individual teeth.

In addition, it was possible to take occlusal views which show the teeth in cross-section. In this case, a slightly larger film, approximately 6×8 cm, is placed on the biting surfaces of the teeth and the cone is placed above the nose, pointing downwards in the case of the upper teeth and upwards from below the chin in the case of the lower teeth.

Large cephalometric films were taken in both the lateral and frontal directions. These showed the detailed anatomy of the skull. Adequate views of the molar teeth which could not be reached easily intraorally were taken by the lateral oblique method. In this method, the cone is placed at the opposite angle of the jaw and an oblique shot is taken of the molars on the other side of the dental arch. In this way, Mrs Ashington was able to build up a complete picture of Natsef-Amun's dentition along with detailed views of the jaw bones, facial skeleton, neck and skull vault. This set of radiographs must comprise a uniquely detailed dental view of a mummy from this era. The excellent preservation of his teeth and jaws means that the set of radiographs taken in 1991 give as accurate a picture of his dentition as if they had been taken on the day he died.

In common with the majority of mummies, Natsef-Amun shows no signs of having received dental treatment. However, at least one of his molar teeth was lost before he died and it may be that it was extracted or that it became so loose that it simply dropped out. There is generalized moderate chronic periodontal bone loss which is a sign that he had chronic periodontal disease. Several of the molar teeth (37, 46, 47 and 48) show periodontal loss involvement which affects the furcations of their roots, i.e. the bone loss has occurred to a more severe degree. The attrition which is described in the section of the visual examination is evident throughout the entire dentition. The enamel has been lost from his teeth and the dentine is exposed. There has been a good build-up of secondary dentine so that the pulp

International Dental Charting

RIGHT SIDE													LEFT SIDE	
Molars			Premolars		Canine		Upper Incisors			Canine	Premolars			Molars
18	17	16	15	14	13	12	11	21	22	23	24	25	26	27	28
48	47	46	45	44	43	42	41	31	32	33	34	35	36	37	38
Molars			Premolars		Canine		Lower Incisors			Canine	Premolars			Molars

chambers of all his teeth have shrunk back. Several of his teeth have calculus (tartar), a mineral deposit which builds up on teeth and speeds the process of periodontal disease.

In addition to the chronic periodontal bone loss there is evidence of infection affecting the bone around several teeth (16, 23, 24, 37). When the membrane around each tooth first becomes chronically inflamed, the periodontal membrane space widens and this is evident in all his lower anterior teeth (particularly 15, 13). This is called early chronic periodontitis. The trabecular pattern of the jaw bone and the skull vault is normal and there is no evidence of osteoporosis or other metabolic or endocrinal bone changes.

Medicine was already specialized when Natsef-Amun was living. As a result of the practice of mummification the ancient Egyptian had a knowledge of anatomy. There are several medical papyri which give information about illnesses and their treatment. The Ebers Papyrus, which is in the University Museum in Leipzig, gives eleven dental prescriptions. These medicaments are all for topical application. One example is for a loose tooth and is a mixture of crushed seeds, ochre and honey, made into a paste and applied to the loose tooth. For toothache, a paste of vegetable and mineral materials with honey is recommended. For inflammation of the gums the prescription is date and beans, exposed to the dew and mixed with milk. This was to be chewed and spat out. All the medicaments are for the treatment of loose teeth and gum disease. There is no prescription for dental decay in the papyrus. This may be because dental decay was relatively uncommon, and tended to be mild. Dental extractions could frequently have been carried out relatively easily, as the teeth were often loose. They would have given instant relief from severe pain and allowed immediate drainage of infection which would have prevented the rise in temperature of a fever and possible septicaemia and osteomyelitis.

The only evidence of restorative dentistry, as yet, was discovered by Junker at Giza and dates from the 4th or 5th Dynasty. This was two molar teeth tied together with gold wire. It was at first thought that this was to support two mobile teeth in the mouth of a living person, but it is now considered that it was added *post mortem* so that the mummy would be as complete as possible for the afterlife.

10 The Histological Examination of Mummified Tissue

E. Tapp

Histology is the study of the microscopic structure of tissues. These may be of plant or animal origin but the present work is concerned largely with the latter. All animal tissues are made up of cells between which are ground substances holding the cells together. In the ground substances there may be different types of fibres and these with the ground substance make up the connective tissue of the body. The cells may vary considerably in size and shape in different organs and it is by studying the pattern of these variations in the cells and their relationship to the connective tissue that a particular organ can be identified.

In disease these patterns alter and other cells often infiltrate the tissues. The study of these changes in tissue caused by disease is known as histopathology. Workers in this field are involved in studying the development and natural history of the disease processes. The tissue studied in this way by the histopathologist may be derived from post-mortem examination or from specimens removed at the operating theatre by surgeons who require the pathologist to determine the particular disease which is present.

The same basic techniques may be used to study the normal structure of mummified tissue and the changes produced in the tissue by mummification as well as to examine it for evidence of disease. Clearly some of the techniques may require modification, as will be discussed later.

When fresh tissue is removed from the body and its blood

supply cut off, enzymes are released from the cells in the tissue which result in alterations of its structure and eventually in its destruction. In order to study the tissue before this can happen it is necessary to kill these enzymes. This may be done by putting the tissue in a variety of liquids but the most commonly used is a solution of formaldehyde made up as 10 per cent formol saline. This process is known as fixing the tissue. The mechanism by which mummified tissue is preserved may appear at first sight to be quite different from fixing the tissue in the way which has just been described. In fact it is basically very similar; in mummification the tissue enzymes are not killed by a chemical but are prevented from destroying the tissue by removal of the water from the tissue, enzymes being able to function only in the presence of water.

When preparing mummified tissue for histological examination it is first necessary to replace the water in the tissue, which then swells up and regains something of its normal appearance. Various methods have been used by workers in the past to rehydrate mummified tissue, most of them involving mixtures of water, sodium carbonate and alcohol. Once the water has been put back into mummified tissue, the tissue will start to degenerate unless fixed. To combat this, a technique has been developed by the present workers which allows water to be introduced gradually into the mummified tissue while at the same time causing fixation to occur. This is achieved by the simple expedient of placing the tissue in a weak solution of formol saline and gradually increasing the strength over a few days until it is finally fixed in the normal solution of 10 per cent formol saline.

Once the mummified tissue has been reconstituted and fixed, the next processes are designed to enable the cutting of thin sections, about 5 microns thick, suitable for examination under the microscope. Two quite different methods can be used, both of which are designed to hold the tissues together whilst they are cut by a sharp knife fixed in a machine known as a microtome. In one method the tissue is frozen into a solid block. This method was used more than 80 years ago by Shattock (1909) to examine the aorta of the Pharaoh Menephtah. It is a particularly useful technique when studying the fats in tissue since these are normally dissolved out by the solutions used in the other main method of processing tissue. This involves surrounding the tissue in paraffin wax. The wax is heated until it is liquid and then allowed to set with the tissue embedded in it. A modification of this method which is particularly suitable for friable mummified tissue is known as double-embedding; here the tissue is immersed in nitrocellulose before being embedded in the paraffin wax. Once the sections are cut, the wax is dissolved away and the sections returned through a series of alcoholic solutions to an aqueous medium in which the sections can be stained.

Staining enables the structure of the tissue to be seen more clearly under the microscope. The various dyes which are used are selected because of their known ability to pick out various parts of the tissues or cells. The combination used most commonly to identify the cells in a tissue for routine surgical purposes involves haematoxylin, which stains the nuclei, and eosin, which stains the cytoplasm. However, difficulty with these stains has been encountered in mummified tissue by some workers; in particular it has been reported that the nuclei of the cells are difficult to stain with haematoxylin (Tapp, 1979). This is probably due to breakdown of the nucleic acids, as it is to these acidic radicles that the haematoxylin normally attaches itself in the process of staining the nuclei. However, with care and persistence there is no doubt that nuclei often can be stained. They have been seen clearly in tissue taken from the epidermis of the skin, and nuclei in other mummified tissues, including liver and cartilage, have also been demonstrated by the present workers. However, as will be seen later, even when the nuclei do not stain with haematoxylin, their presence may be demonstrated with the electron microscope.

The next most commonly used group of stains are those which attach themselves to the connective tissues of the body. These are particularly useful in mummified tissue, for whilst the cells in the tissue may have degenerated and be no longer visible, the connective tissues such as the reticulin, collagen and muscle fibres are more resistant to post-mortem change. As they form the framework of the tissue, their persistence enables the identification of the tissue; and as this framework is often distorted when the tissue is affected by disease, any alteration to their pattern may allow the presence of disease to be detected.

One of the most frequently used connective tissue stains is that of Van Gieson. With this method, collagen stains red and muscle yellow. It is often combined with the Verhoeff stain which dyes elastic fibres black. This combination shows up the structure of blood vessels particularly well and assists identification of the presence of disease in them.

An alternative to Van Gieson is the Masson trichrome technique, whereby collagen is stained green and muscle red. When this stain is used on the connective tissue of skin and subcutaneous tissue from some mummies, a change in the normal staining pattern has been observed by Tapp (1984), the collagen in the more superficial part staining red, whilst that in the deeper parts stains normally. This reversal of the normal stain-

Fig. 45 *The Two Brothers were the first mummies to be scientifically investigated in Manchester, when they were the subject of an examination by Dr Margaret Murray in 1908*

ing pattern in the superficial part of the skin may well be due to the materials used in embalming infiltrating the outer layers of the skin. Natron with its combination of various salts might well alter the staining properties of collagen in this way.

The muscular tissues of the body are of two types. So-called smooth muscle is found in structures such as blood vessels and the intestine. This type of muscle is not under the control of the will. On the other hand, striated muscle, which forms the muscles of the skeleton and is under voluntary control, has a particular structure which gives the appearance of striations under the microscope. These may be seen with the Masson trichrome technique, but another stain, phosphotungstic acid haematoxylin, shows these striations particularly well. The ability to see the striations in mummified tissue naturally depends on the degree of preservation but the present workers have been able to demonstrate them on several occasions. Samples of muscle from Egyptian mummies are always worth examining in detail as they may reveal evidence of disease. In particular, some worm infestations may persist in encysted forms in voluntary muscle and these can be demonstrated with the stains outlined above.

Nerves may also be identified in the subcutaneous tissue and elsewhere in the body with these connective tissue stains. The latter show up the fibrous capsule and the septa which divide the nerve into separate compartments, but more specialized stains are necessary to identify the components of the nerve fibres.

Connective tissue stains such as the Gordon and Sweet technique which show up reticulin fibres are particularly effective in demonstrating the overall structure of a tissue and have been useful in some cases. In particular, using this method it was possible to show that the liver found in the canopic jar belonging to Nekht-Ankh (one of the Two Brothers) had a normal structure. It will be seen later that the electron microscope showed the presence of a liver fluke infestation in this liver. This condition may lead to scarring or even cirrhosis but clearly the disease had not progressed to this state in the case of Nekht-Ankh.

Other stains which may be useful in mummified tissue are those for detecting bacteria and fungi. The Gram stain is widely used in hospital practice to detect bacteria and although these may occur as post-mortem contaminants in many mummified tissues, it is always worth while staining mummified tissue in this way. Fungi may be detected with silver stains and are seen as moulds growing into the skin of mummies. Most of these originate from the time of mummification, their spread stopping when the tissues have been sufficiently dehydrated. However, some fungal infestations may be the result of inadequate conservation in more recent times.

The methods of staining mummified tissues which have been discussed so far are empirical and the mechanism of the staining reaction is incompletely understood in most cases. Those stains which have a clear chemical base for their reaction are known as histochemical stains and it is interesting that, although the tissues of Egyptian mummies are some two thousand or more years old, it is still possible in some cases to get the chemical reactions to work. One of the most striking examples found by the present workers was the staining of mucins in the intestinal cells of mummified tissue with the Periodic Acid Schiff reaction. Mucins which are found in cartilage may also be stained with this technique and when it is combined with alcian blue it is possible to detect two quite different mucins within this tissue.

A further histochemical stain which has been used in Egyptian mummies is the Perls' reaction for staining iron pigment. Iron is often deposited in the tissues following injuries as a result of blood escaping from the tissue and then breaking down and releasing iron. Its presence may therefore be a marker for old trauma. In addition, there are some diseases such as haemochromatosis which result in excess iron being deposited in the tissues; this can lead to cirrhosis of the liver and diabetes mellitus. Clearly it is useful to check mummified tissue for this pigment.

Whilst the histochemical stains allow a limited number of chemical substances in cells to be identified, the development of immunohistochemistry during the past fifteen years has led to great improvements in the identification of cell constituents. Rather than relying on a chemical reaction between the dye and the substance to be stained, these methods involve an immunological reaction between the two. The reactions depend on the ability of animals to produce a substance (antibody) when a material (antigen) which is foreign to that animal is introduced to it. The antibody–antigen reaction is a very specific one and hence any staining method based on it will allow the specific identification of the substance targeted by the antibody. A wide range of antibodies to human antigens has been produced in other animals and these antibodies are available to be linked with a dye so that when they are applied to tissues they stain the specific antigen in the tissue. The present workers have used these stains on mummified tissue and, despite the age of the tissues, some promising results have been obtained (Krypczyk and Tapp, 1986). One of the earliest of these was the discovery that it is possible to stain the outer horny layer of mummified skin in this way.

Muscle contains a substance called myoglobin and the identification of this protein in tumours derived from muscle may allow the pathologist to make a positive diagnosis in cases where routine stains have resulted in some doubt as to the true nature of a tumour. In some instances this may be important in the treatment of the tumour. In the same way, the identification of myoglobin in otherwise poorly preserved mummified tissue allows a positive identification of the tissue. The use of other newer immunohistochemical stains for connective tissue elements such as vimentin and desmin should also be explored in mummified tissue.

Antibodies to a substance known as carcinoembryonic antigen which, as the name suggests, occurs in certain cancers as well as in embryonic tissue is now available. It is found widely in the intestine of man and it has been shown that it can still be identified in mummified intestine (Tapp, 1984).

A further interesting use of immunohistochemical stains involves the brain. The latter is one of the first tissues to break down after death and so it is not surprising to find that cells could not be identified in mummified brain tissue. However, an antibody to one of the substances found in brain cells known as glial fibrillary acidic protein is available and has been used to identify it in mummified brain, even though the individual cells which originally contained the material cannot be recognized. Work is now in progress on the use of other immunohistochemical stains for substances found in the brain and in nerve fibres; that for neurofilaments is particularly promising.

The histological methods outlined so far involve light microscopy. If the histologist wishes to examine tissue at a magnification greater than 800 times normal size it is necessary to use the electron microscope. Here electrons are used instead of visible light and electromagnets replace the glass lenses used in the light microscope. The degree of detail which can be discerned by a microscope is called the resolving power and this is related inversely to the wavelength of the irradiation used to illuminate the specimen. As electrons exhibit wave properties with a wavelength which is a fraction of that of visible light, the electron microscope allows much greater resolution of the detailed structure of the cells in the specimen, as well as enabling magnifications of many thousand times to be achieved.

There are three main types of electron microscope. The transmission electron microscope is used rather like a light microscope. Very thin sections of tissue are prepared and a beam of electrons directed through them to produce an image on a screen. Although these microscopes have been available for some forty years, it was only in the late 1960s that the first attempts were made by Lewin (1967) to examine the ultrastructure of Egyptian mummies. It is likely that other workers have been discouraged from attempting to examine mummified tissue at a subcellular level because it is known that the contents of cells undergo rapid deterioration unless they are fixed soon after being removed from the living body. However, the experience of Lewin and then Hufnagel (1973) encouraged the present workers to study a wide range of mummified tissues and, as will be seen below, quite remarkable detail of the structures within the cells can still be identified in some cases (Curry, Anfield and Tapp, 1979; Krypczyk and Tapp, 1986).

The liver was one of the first tissues to be examined. The cell membranes were well preserved and desmosomes could be identified. The latter are areas of intimate cell contact where cell-to-cell communication takes place. The cytoplasm of the cells showed electron-lucent areas which were about the size of mitochondria and these probably indicate the position of these organelles prior to their disintegration. The nuclei in the liver cells had been difficult to stain in sections prepared for the light microscope, but with the electron microscope rather shrunken nuclei could be identified in most of the cells. Centrioles were identified in two cells. The presence of these organelles indicates that these cells were undergoing division at the time when the ancient Egyptian died. Liver cells produce bile and this is collected in small canaliculi between the cells prior to flowing into larger ducts and then eventually into the gall bladder. The canaliculi could be recognized between the cells in the mummified liver although the microvilli, minute finger-like protrusions of the cell wall involved in the production of bile, had disintegrated.

The skin has also been examined and again the subcellular detail that has been revealed is surprising. Keratin could be seen in the outer horny layer of the skin. In the deeper layers, desmosomes with attached tonofilaments, features of keratin-producing cells, can be identified. As under the light microscope, a feature of the skin and many other tissues was the presence of micro-organisms. Some of these were filamentous and were probably fungal hyphae, whilst others were spherical and almost certainly bacterial cocci. It has been stressed already that many of the micro-organisms seen in mummified tissue are contaminants and not a manifestation of disease in the mummy. In addition, bacteria with a complex envelope comprised of many concentric layers were also seen. These bacterial spores represent bacteria in a resting phase. Such spores may exist in this dormant stage for many years and then produce disease later, when the conditions are favourable. This has to be borne in mind during the examination of Egyptian mummies and whilst the 'curse of the mummies' which was said to affect earlier workers who opened tombs is largely to be discounted, it is interesting to note that some of the respiratory diseases suffered by excavators soon after opening tombs may be due to the fungal infestation known as histoplasmosis. The spores of this organism are found in bat droppings and it is likely that inhalation of dust containing spores derived from this source was the cause of the infection in these people.

Examination of intestine under the electron microscope showed once again, as with the liver, that nuclei which do not stain in ordinary sections can be identified with the electron microscope. In this case well-preserved nuclei were seen in the cells around the lumen of a gland. Moreover, prominent nucleoli could be identified within the nuclei.

The ultrastructure of voluntary muscle has also been examined. Better preserved samples in which cross-striations were identifiable with the light microscope showed longitudinally arranged fibrils with a cross-banding pattern but did not display the organized regular cross-banding sequence seen in fresh tissue. They also showed electron-lucent vacuoles between the fibres possibly indicating the location of mitochondria.

Examination of lung tissue with the electron microscope did not show any residual cells but the scarring observed with the light microscope in the lung of Nekht-Ankh could be resolved electronoptically into collagen and elastic fibres. This scarring was associated with particles which were found to have a crystalline structure. These were examined further with the second type of electron microscope known as the analytical microscope, which produces an analysis of the elements in the tissue. This proved to be very useful in the examination of the particles from Nekht-Ankh's lung. A high proportion of silicone, iron and titanium was discovered in the crystals. These findings helped to establish the diagnosis of sand pneumoconiosis in this case.

A further use of the analytical microscope has been to examine mummified tissue for heavy metals. The accumulation in the body of small quantities of metals such as lead and mercury is believed to be a consequence of living in our industrial society and indeed poisoning with these metals may occur as the result of inadequate disposal of industrial waste. In ancient Egypt these factors are less likely to have been important but the possibility of deliberate poisoning has to be considered. With this in mind lung, liver, intestine and brain tissue from mummies have been examined with the analytical electron microscope. All the tissues showed a complete absence of lead, mercury or other heavy metals (Curry, Anfield and Tapp, 1979). It is possible that very small amounts of these elements could be dissolved out in processing the tissue, but these findings certainly suggest that if there were any heavy metals present at all they were in a much lower concentration than is found in modern populations. This finding is in keeping with that of Cockburn and his co-workers (1975) who found low levels of lead in two Egyptian mummies. However, the same worker found that the level of mercury in Pum I and Pum II was similar to that in modern man. Clearly this is an interesting field which deserves further attention.

The scanning electron microscope is the third type which has been used in the study of ancient Egyptian material. This machine is used to examine the surface of solid objects. A fine beam of electrons is made to scan the specimen and an image is built up sequentially on a cathode ray tube just as in the formation of the picture on the television screen. The images produced in this way are quite remarkably clear and have a good depth of field.

This microscope has been used in the past to study the hair of Egyptian mummies and it was thought that this technique might be of value in elucidating the race of the Egyptian mummies in the Manchester collection known as the Two Brothers (Curry,

Anfield and Tapp, 1979). There has been considerable specu-lation concerning the parentage of these two mummies: their sarcophagi depict one as being negroid and the other semitic, but the coffin inscriptions indicate that they both had the same mother. Fortunately, when Margaret Murray unwrapped these mummies in 1908 she kept samples of their hair. After coating some of them with gold they were examined under the scanning electron microscope. All the samples examined showed an identical structure, the outer surface of the hair being covered by the same type of scales, suggesting that the Two Brothers were of the same race.

The other main field in which the scanning electron micro-scope has been used is in the examination of the various insects which have been found in the Manchester Museum collection of mummies. These insects were studied by Curry (1979) who found that most of them were either beetles (Coleoptera) or true flies (Diptera). As Curry has pointed out, it is difficult to determine precisely when these insects got into the mummies. Beetles could invade the body at any time from death through to when the mummy is on display in a museum, but the larval stages of flies require a moist food source and therefore the time of infestation with flies is easier to deduce. Since fly larvae go through various stages of development at known times, the recognition of these forms may allow forensic scientists to deduce the time of death.

Mummy 1770 contained many insects, the commonest being the beetle known as *Necrobia rufipes* and a fly called *Piophilia casei*. The puparia of the fly were more numerous in the inner bandages and body of the mummy than in the outer layers of bandage. These findings may be related to the suggestion that the body of Mummy 1770 had been rehydrated, perhaps by flooding of the tomb, and then rewrapped.

Different insects were found in the Two Brothers. Puparia of the fly *Chrysomyia albiceps* were common whilst the predomi-nant beetle was the hump spider beetle, *Gibbum psylloides*. The latter is a serious pest of vegetable products and may have used the bandages of Nekht-Ankh and his brother Khnum-Nakht as a food source. A complete description of the findings and their interpretation are given in Curry's paper which illustrates the use of the scanning electron microscope in this field very well.

It will be seen from the above that, with certain minor modifications, the techniques of histology can be applied in the study of mummified tissue. Of course, the utmost care must be taken in handling the specimens during processing and a good deal of skill is required to obtain adequate sections. Experimentation with the routine stains can ultimately give satisfactory results although there may be some variation in the

Fig. 46 *These glass jars contain fragments of tissue which had been removed from the Two Brothers at the time of the unwrapping and had been preserved in the museum from that time*

staining characteristics of collagen close to the surface of the skin which may be related to the mummification procedure.

Histochemical and immunohistochemical stains, which are much more specific in their staining characteristics, have been surprisingly successful in detecting individual substances within mummified tissue. It is clear from this that many of these may remain unchanged chemically and immunologically for several thousand years.

The transmission electron microscope allows additional resolution and much greater magnification to be obtained. It can be used successfully on mummified tissue and the quite remarkable preservation of subcellular structures in these tissues can be demonstrated.

The analytical electron microscope has also been useful in detecting the structure of crystalline particles in the lung of one mummy and in measuring the levels of heavy metals in mummified tissue. No evidence of environmental pollution or deliberate poisoning has been detected.

Finally, the scanning electron microscope may be used to examine the surface of solid materials. It has been shown that it has a place in the study of mummified hair as well as in the examination of the many insects found within mummies and their wrappings.

In the next chapter it will be seen how these techniques have been used in the examination of the tissues from the Leeds Mummy as well as in the determination of disease in Egyptian mummies.

11

The Autopsy and Endoscopy of The Leeds Mummy

E. Tapp and K. Wildsmith

The previous chapter established that it is possible to obtain satisfactory histological sections of mummified tissue and to examine these by both light and electronmicroscopy for evidence of disease.

Material for these studies may be obtained from several sources. Small pieces may be cut off an intact mummy without spoiling it as a museum exhibit or indeed interfering with any further investigations on the mummy which might be required as techniques develop in the future. Specimens of skin and structures found immediately beneath the skin, such as fat, muscle, nerves and blood vessels, can be obtained in this way and may be a fruitful source of material for histological and histopathological examination.

A second source of material are the organs which were removed from the body by ancient Egyptians and preserved in canopic jars as part of the mummification ritual. A particularly interesting example of such a specimen was found in one of the canopic jars belonging to Nekht-Ankh. The organ was wrapped in bandages but when these had been partly removed it could be recognized with the naked eye as having the basic structure of the liver. Even more revealing, however, was a rounded mass which protruded from one edge. This was the gall bladder, a thin-walled bag which lies close to the anterior border of the liver and which stores the bile produced by the liver until this is released into the intestine to assist with the digestion.

The histological and electronoptical structure of this liver has been described in the previous chapter, but more interesting from the pathologist's point of view was the presence under the electron microscope of a group of flattened cells with thickened walls. This structure is believed to be the remains of a liver fluke, *Fasciola hepatica*. This is a worm that is found commonly in sheep, goats and cattle but may also infect man.

The eggs of the worm are passed in the faeces of the infected animal and hatch in water, where they enter an intermediate life cycle in snails. Immature forms escape from the snails and form small cysts on the plants which grow in the water. When these plants are eaten the cysts are digested and the freed larvae make their way to the liver. Here they develop into adult forms which may cause fibrosis and ultimately liver failure. Clearly human infestation will occur when vegetables are grown in polluted water and in these days the most common source of this infection is watercress. In ancient Egypt the swampy ground following the inundation would have been an excellent site for the proliferation of the snails. As the latter play an important role in the spread of the disease, any crops grown under these conditions would have been heavily infested with the cysts and an important source of infection to man. It appears, however, that this is the first instance of such infection being found in Egyptian mummies.

Researchers are not always so fortunate as to find intact organs in canopic jars but sometimes jars which appear to be empty on first sight do contain small fragments of tissue. These may yield fruitful results and are always worth examining under the microscope.

A third source of material are the organs which the ancient Egyptians did not put into canopic jars but which were left within the wrappings of the mummy after mummification. Clearly this had occurred in the case of Asru (Fig. 47). This mummy was unwrapped several years ago and a package was found at that time lying between her legs (Tapp, 1979a). When the bandages were removed from this package the contents did not appear to be particularly interesting. However, under the microscope, it was seen quite clearly to be part of the small intestine; more-over, there were many developing forms of a worm called strongyloides in the wall. Infection with this worm usually occurs when the feet are exposed to water or mud containing immature forms of the worm. The latter penetrate the feet and pass via veins to the heart and ultimately through the lungs into the airways. After migrating up the windpipe they are swal-

Fig. 47 *The mummy of Asru, a Chantress of Amun in the Temple of Karnak, who lived during the 25th Dynasty (about 600 BC). When her mummy was unwrapped, a package of mummified viscera was found between her thighs*

lowed and mature into adult forms in the intestine. The eggs of these adults are then passed into the faeces and complete the circle by getting into the water. Clearly this type of infestation, like the liver fluke, would have been a major problem in ancient Egypt where the farmer could only plant his fields at the time of the inundation. Interestingly, such infestations remain a problem at present and manual workers can still be seen exposing themselves to this kind of infection by paddling in the irrigation canals without any form of protection on the hands or feet.

It is clear that some of the sources mentioned so far have led to the discovery of disease in Egyptian mummies, but a good deal of a histopathologist's work involves post-mortem examinations. During these examinations some diseases of the body can be seen with the naked eye whilst others are only diagnosed when tissue from the autopsy has been examined under the microscope. It is to this source that a histopathologist will naturally turn in his investigation of disease in ancient Egypt.

It will naturally be appreciated that Egyptian mummies are invaluable antiquities which cannot be replaced if destroyed and clearly there are limits to the number of mummies which may be examined in this way. There must also be limits to the extent of the autopsy in individual mummies. In addition, tissue obtained at autopsies on Egyptian mummies should be carefully preserved, in case new techniques are developed in the future which allow further information to be obtained from them.

These guidelines have been constantly borne in mind during

the work on Egyptian mummies in Manchester and it is hoped that this will be illustrated in the following description of the three post-mortem examinations which have been carried out there. The most recent of these is, of course, the Leeds Mummy, the subject of the present multidisciplinary investigation.

The first mummies to be investigated scientifically in Manchester were the Two Brothers in 1908. These mummies were discovered in an unopened tomb at Rifeh. They were excavated by Sir Flinders Petrie and subsequently donated to the Manchester Museum by the British School of Archaeology in Egypt. The unwrapping and dissection of the mummies is described by Margaret Murray in her book *Tomb of the Two Brothers* (1910). It is clear both from her description and from the photographs taken at the time that the tissues of the mummies were poorly preserved and it was not possible to recognize individual organs. However, Margaret Murray had the foresight to keep several of the fragments which broke away from the mummy as she carried out the unwrapping. Consequently tissue was available for histological examination many years later.

Several different tissues were identified amongst the fragments, but it was the examination of pieces of lung which proved to be particularly interesting. Under the microscope the lungs showed marked scarring and the presence of fine particles of sand or stone. This condition, known as sand pneumoconiosis, is similar to that seen in coal miners and stonemasons whose lungs are damaged by the inhalation of fine dust. (Tapp, Curry and Anfield, 1975). However, the inscription on the tomb furniture of Nekht-Ankh indicates that he was a priest rather than a stonemason and indeed it is believed that the disease, from which Nekht-Ankh and other ancient Egyptians suffered, originated from their natural environment in which sandstorms were common and in which fine particles of sand would have been inhaled. Interestingly, a similar condition has been described in modern desert populations of the Negev and Sahara.

Following the unwrapping of the Two Brothers there was a gap of some seventy years before the next autopsy on an Egyptian mummy was carried out in Manchester. This was the unwrapping and post-mortem examination of Mummy 1770 in 1975, the first mummy to be investigated in this way in modern times (Tapp, 1979b; 1986). Mummy 1770 came to the Manchester Museum in about 1896. The source of the mummy is not known with certainty, but an entry in the diary of Sir Flinders Petrie and a letter he sent to a friend after a visit to Manchester suggests that it came from his excavations at Hawara in Middle Egypt. It was thought from the external wrappings that the mummy originated in the Greek or Roman Period.

The mummy had been examined radiologically some years before and the x-rays showed that the body was that of a child about fourteen years old. They also revealed a good deal of damage to the head and neck of the mummy as well as showing that parts of the legs were missing, the right leg having been amputated through the thigh bone and the left through the shin bone. At autopsy it was found that the right leg had been splinted to an artificial leg to make it roughly the same length as the left and an artificial foot made from reeds and mud had been attached to it.

During the course of the unwrapping, gold nipple covers and gold finger stalls were found, indicating that the child was of high rank, but a puzzling feature was the absence of any name on the mummy case (Fig. 48). Moreover, it had been assumed from the mummy case that the body was that of a girl and consequently it was some surprise when the autopsy revealed the presence of an artificial phallus. A further unusual feature at autopsy was the presence of resin in the joint cavities and between the bones of the spine, although this was absent from the outer parts of the mummy and its wrappings.

Modern techniques made these strange findings more understandable, for it was discovered by carbon dating that the bandages were about a thousand years younger than the body. These findings indicated that the child had probably died 1200 BC but had been rewrapped in the Greek or Roman Period. There is evidence that some royal mummies of the 20th or 21st dynasties were moved to new tombs at a much later date and it is possible that 1770 was one of these. The Egyptians would not necessarily have known whom they were unwrapping, hence the lack of identification. On the other hand they would have known that it was someone of importance and this would explain the careful reconstruction of the legs and feet, as well as the gold nipple covers and finger stalls. It is possible, moreover, that they did not know the sex of the child when they were rewrapping it and therefore played safe by providing it with an artificial phallus as well as the gold nipple covers. The finding of resin in the deeper parts of the mummy may also be explained by a rewrapping, resin being used in the initial mummification of the body but not when it was rewrapped some thousand years later.

The amputated ends of the thigh and shin bones are rather irregular and the amputations do not appear to have been carried out surgically, although it is believed that such procedures were known in ancient Egypt (Fig. 49). Moreover, examination of the ends of the bones under the microscope did

Fig. 48 *These golden finger stalls found on Mummy 1770 were placed over the fingernails. They were tied down with cotton to keep the fingernails in position so that they would be intact for the afterlife*

Fig. 49 *The amputated end of the thigh bone of Mummy 1770 is irregular and appears to be the result of the leg being broken off rather than being amputated surgically*

Fig. 50 *The tail of a Guinea worm emerging from an ulcer on the foot. Eggs can now escape from this to contaminate water and so complete the life cycle of the worm*

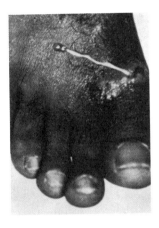

not reveal any evidence of healing, indicating that the amputations were carried out either after death or at the most a week or two prior to death. Various suggestions have been made as to how the legs came to be amputated, including a possible road traffic accident involving a chariot. The irregular indentations in the ends of the bones have also been likened to teeth marks and consideration has been given as to whether the legs were bitten off by a crocodile. This is unlikely as crocodiles tend to take hold of a limb and disarticulate it at a joint by shaking the rest of the body from the limb.

A further finding at autopsy was a hard nodule about 2 cm across in the anterior abdominal wall which may well be connected with the amputations. X-rays of this nodule showed it to be the remains of a Guinea worm, *Dracunculus medinensis*, which had become impregnated with calcium salts. Infection with this worm occurs when drinking water containing immature forms of the worm is swallowed. The immature forms burrow through the wall of the stomach and develop into adults in the anterior abdominal wall. The adult female is about a metre long whilst the male is only a matter of centimetres. Copulation occurs in the abdominal wall and then the male dies. It is clear that the calcified worm in the anterior abdominal wall of Mummy 1770 is the remains of the male worm and that this worm had died some months before Mummy 1770 as we know that calcification of the dead worm would take this length of time to occur.

The pregnant female burrows its way through the subcutaneous tissues of the body and usually ends up in one of the legs where it causes ulceration of the skin. The tail of the worm protrudes through the ulcer and the eggs contaminate water, so completing the cycle (Fig. 50). One method of treating this worm infestation was to grab the tail of the worm in a cleft stick as it protruded through the ulcer and wrap it around the stick. A short segment of the worm was then extracted each day until it had been removed completely. Unfortunately if the worm broke during this procedure, a marked inflammatory response occurred in the tissue and this in some instances could result in the affected leg having to be amputated. However, one can only speculate as to whether or not this is the explanation for Mummy 1770 losing parts of her legs.

It has been pointed out already that the number of autopsies of the type carried out on Mummy 1770 which results in destruction of the mummy must of necessity be extremely limited. Consequently during the next few years attempts were made to find means whereby tissues of Egyptian mummies could be obtained and examined without destroying the mummy, or indeed without affecting its appearance in any way since this would limit its future use for display purposes.

At first attempts were made to obtain tissues from mummies using the types of needles which are employed by doctors to take small samples of liver and kidney from living individuals without the necessity for the patient to undergo open surgery. Unfortunately, these methods depend to a large extent on the tissues flowing into the needle and so were not successful in obtaining samples of mummified tissue.

Subsequently a needle with a bore of 0.5 cm was obtained and with this cores of tissue could occasionally be removed from the inside of Egyptian mummies. However, the method was somewhat of a hit-and-miss procedure and it was only when experiments with endoscopes began that it was realized that these instruments provided a method of examining the inside of body cavities of mummies, as well as enabling samples to be taken from internal organs for histological examinations (Tapp, Stanworth and Wildsmith, 1984).

The original endoscopes consisted of a simple tube illuminated by a light reflected down the tube by a mirror. Later an electric bulb was incorporated into the probing end of the endoscope but this together with the wide bore of the instrument made endoscopy a very uncomfortable procedure for the patient. In the 1950s, however, fibre-optic instruments were developed, in which both the light and the image of the object being viewed were transmitted along fine strands of glass. This development has allowed flexible endoscopes to be made with working lengths of up to 2.5 m and diameters as small as 2.4 mm. The probing tip of these instruments can be manipulated by controls at the proximal end so that it points in any direction, giving excellent control over the examination. Rigid endoscopes are also used. These have a shorter working length (to about 50 cm) but have the advantage that they can be obtained with diameters as small as 1.7 mm. Further developments of the optics used in endoscopes now allow photographs to be taken through them. In Manchester sophisticated video cameras have been used which enable the endoscopic findings to be recorded and subsequently re-examined at will.

In medicine, endoscopes are used by physicians to examine the inside of the gullet, stomach and intestines for ulcers which could be cancers and by urological surgeons to examine the bladder for evidence of tumours. Such examinations, which allow direct viewing of the parts and also enable small specimens to be taken for histological examination, often avoid the need for patients to have major surgery.

In Egyptian mummies the normal orifices through which endoscopes can be introduced into the body are usually closed. However, it has been possible to examine the mouth and back of the throat, as well as the lower parts of the rectum, in some cases, and although the usual routes used in examination of patients are not available in Egyptian mummies, the methods used by ancient Egyptian embalmers have sometimes provided a route through which an endoscope can be introduced. In particular, the method used by the embalmers to remove the brain through the base of the skull and nose has provided a satisfactory pathway whereby an endoscope can be introduced into the skull.

As the end of the endoscope passes through the nasal passages, the defect in the base of the skull produced by the ancient Egyptian embalmers can be seen and when the endoscope reaches the cavity there is a good view of the anterior part of the latter. Both the inside of the skull bones and the membranes lining them can be examined and, if necessary, biopsied. If part of the brain has been left behind by the embalmers, samples of this can also be removed for examination under the microscope.

The probing end of the endoscope can also be directed backwards to examine the rest of the cavity including the pituitary fossa. This contains a gland whose hormones control many of the functions of the body. In some instances, the tip of the endoscope can be passed backwards far enough to allow the upper part of the spinal canal to be examined.

Histological examination of brain tissue and nerves removed in this way has enabled the degree of post-mortem change in the brain to be studied and in particular the change we call adipocere (Thompson, Lynch and Tapp, 1986). This is the term used to describe tissues which have not broken down after death and have taken on a waxy appearance. Further reference to this will be made when tissues from the Leeds Mummy are discussed.

Histological examination of brain tissue obtained by endoscopy from Mummy 22940 has shown the presence of a hydatid cyst in this isolated mummy head. Hydatid disease is the result of infection with the dog tape worm, which usually only affects dogs and sheep. However if food for human consumption is contaminated with the eggs of the worm, they can develop in humans. Cysts measuring up to about 5 cm across may develop in several organs including the brain, lung, liver and kidney. In some organs the cyst may remain undiagnosed for several years, but in the brain they act like a brain tumour. As they gradually grow in size within a rigid skull there is ever-increasing pressure on the rest of the brain, resulting in head-ache, blurring of vision and vomiting with eventual loss of consciousness and death. When a particular disease is found in an Egyptian mummy it is unusual to be certain that this caused the person's death, but events are so predictable with hydatid cysts in the brain that, in the case of Mummy 22940, there can be little doubt that this was his cause of death.

The embalmers further assisted the endoscopist by removing the lungs from the chest cavity as well as many of the abdominal organs. This, in many instances, resulted in a space being available in the chest into which an endoscope can be introduced. To enter the chest cavity a small hole is made between the ribs and a rigid endoscope passed into the cavity (Fig. 51). Through this the inside of the chest wall, including the ribs, can be examined. The cavity can also be checked for any remains of the lungs or the presence of the heart, the latter usually being left in the body by the embalmers.

Fig. 51 A rigid endoscope being used to investigate the chest cavity of a mummy, by which means the heart, lungs and ribcage can be examined. If necessary a biopsy can be taken

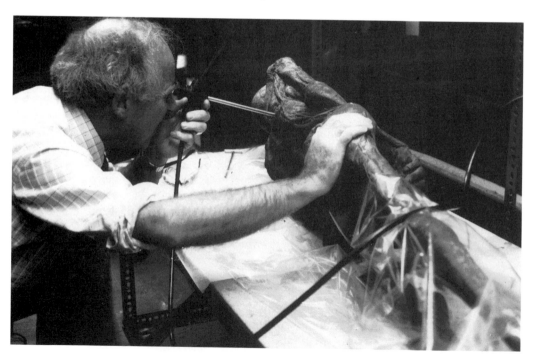

In the Mummy Asru, x-rays had shown what was thought to be either heart or collapsed lung close to the midline of the chest. By using endoscopy, combined with radiological screening of the chest under direct vision, it was possible to manoeuvre the endoscope to this area and to take a sample of the tissue. Histologically it consisted of lung and the sections showed evidence of a collapsed hydatid cyst. Clearly this was a common infestation in ancient Egypt.

The Mummy Khary was still fully bandaged at the time of the examination and, as the normal external landmarks of the body were obscured by this, it provided an even more severe test of the endoscopic techniques. When an endoscope was introduced into the chest cavity in this case, the lungs were only partially collapsed as they were adherent to the inside of the chest wall in some places. These adhesions are caused by inflammation in the lungs, the accompanying inflammatory exudate on the surface of the lungs glueing them to the chest wall. They indicate that Khary had suffered from pleurisy, probably associated with pneumonia, some considerable time before she died. Samples of lung removed through the endoscope in this case showed the typical changes of sand pneumonconiosis and it is clear from these findings and from several other samples of mummy lung tissue which have been examined that this was a widespread condition in ancient Egypt. It is difficult to know how severely the ancient Egyptians were incapacitated by the disease. Certainly the similar condition in stonemasons can be extremely disabling and result in marked breathlessness; and ultimately, many of these patients die from heart failure due to the strain put upon the heart by the damaged lungs.

Clearly the endoscope has provided a useful tool in the examination of intact Egyptian mummies. It will be seen in the study of the Leeds Mummy that it can also be an invaluable adjunct to post-mortem examination.

The original investigation on the Leeds Mummy was carried out in 1828. Anatomical details were recorded, but the techniques for histological examination of tissue at that time were primitive; indeed, the speciality of pathology was in its infancy (Blayds, 1828). It is interesting, therefore, to compare the findings at that time with those of the present examinations and to see how the newer techniques have allowed the earlier findings to be reinterpreted, as well as yielding evidence of disease suffered by Natsef-Amun.

At the original examination the bandages were removed from the face and neck. The ones on the trunk were cut and extensively disturbed. At this time 'a thick layer of spicery', consisting of 'fragrant woods and barks' was present between the bandages and the skin, 'nowhere less than an inch in thickness'.

Clearly this material prevented the skin from sticking to the bandages as it does when mummies have been embalmed with resin. Consequently the bandages could be removed without pulling the skin off the surface of the body. As a result of this the present workers found that to the naked eye the skin appeared to be in good condition, particularly on the face, neck and upper chest (Fig. 52). On the feet, however, where the skin is naturally thick, the outermost horny layer had separated from the underlying epidermis, but histological sections of this horny layer showed it to be well preserved.

The embalming technique did not, unfortunately, preserve the epidermis of the skin; when this was examined under a microscope, the cells of the epidermis had degenerated into an amorphous mass and on the surface of this were the remains of the vegetable matter used in the embalming. However, the structure of the deeper part of the skin or dermis was better preserved. It showed normal staining with the Masson trichrome technique, collagen staining green and muscle staining red. It has been noted previously that this is not always the case with mummified skin and that the reversal in the staining properties of collagen and muscle seen in some cases has been attributed to embalming material soaking into the outer part of the skin (Tapp, Stanworth and Wildsmith, 1984). Clearly this had not occurred with the 'spicery' materials used on the surface of Natsef-Amun.

Returning to the observations made in 1828, it is interesting to note that the skin was described as greasy to the touch and that the skin and underlying flesh had some resemblance to the substance known as 'adipocere'. The question of 'adipocere' was raised again by George (1828) in his chemical examination of some of the substances connected with the mummy. In our examination the skin did not appear to be particularly greasy, but since it had been exposed to the air for 150 years it is not surprising that this greasy appearance had disappeared.

However, it is worth considering the question of adipocere at this point. George (1828) suggested that this greasy material was either 'adipocire' produced by embalming or wax introduced into the tissue during mummification. The former was favoured on the basis that: (a) the bones of the most exposed parts such as the head were not penetrated by the waxy substance, in which it was supposed that body would have been immersed for several days; (b) the wax was not found in greater abundance on or near to the surface than in the more deeply seated parts; and (c) the 'cuticle' or superficial layer of the skin covered every part of the body and this would not have been the case if it had been exposed to an elevated temperature (hot wax). Interestingly, however, he referred to the paper on Egyptian mummies by

Fig. 52 *Material placed between the skin and bandages at mummification had prevented the bandages from sticking to the skin and consequently when they were removed, the skin on the face of Natsef-Amun was intact and in good condition*

Granville (1825) and to his conclusion that wax was employed in the mummification process. It is worth noting that Granville suggests that the word mummy comes from the coptic word for wax, which is *mum*.

We are fortunate that not only is there now a better understanding of the process of adipocere formation but also that it is possible to examine the tissues under the microscope for this. The waxy appearance of tissue known as adipocere is due to the accumulation of fatty acid crystals (chiefly palmitic acid) in the tissues. These crystals, which can be identified in polarized light, are seen quite clearly in the subcutaneous tissue of Natsef-Amun. There can be little doubt therefore that the conclusion reached by George, although based on different premises, was quite correct and that the waxy material seen by the original workers was adipocere.

The crystals of adipocere originate from the breakdown of the neutral fats which are widespread in the body. This breakdown is initiated by bacterial and tissue enzymes released into the tissue after death. As the chemical process is one of hydrolysis, the reaction extracts water from the surrounding tissue and helps to preserve it. In addition, the presence of a high concentration of fatty acids has a preservative effect, the acidity killing off bacteria which might otherwise have produced putrefaction.

The production of adipocere after death has been studied in modern bodies which have been dead for several years, but little has been written of its presence in mummified tissue. It is worth noting, however, that Ruffer (1911) saw small white patches in several of the internal organs of Greek and Roman sand-buried bodies. He likened these to miliary tuberculosis and suggested that they represented adipocere formation, but his techniques did not allow him to confirm this under the microscope. Adipocere has been found, however, in the brain of one mummy in Manchester and its development was attributed in this case to the fact that the residual brain tissue in this mummy had been allowed to undergo 'natural' post-mortem changes. (Thompson, Lynch and Tapp, 1986). Clearly, if a body was mummified soon after death then rapid drying of the body would tend to inhibit adipocere formation since water is required for this process; this may well be the reason for it not being seen commonly in Egyptian mummies.

Returning to the external appearance of the mummy in 1828, it was noted by Blayds that there was some compression of the forehead and bridge of the nose which was attributed to bandages being drawn tightly across the face whilst the tissue was still soft. These markings can still be seen and certainly are compatible with having been produced in this way (Fig. 52).

The nose was examined by Teale and Hey (1828) in some

detail and the passage in the right nostril through which the brain had been removed was identified. Unfortunately the nose has been broken off since that time and is missing. It is likely that this occurred in 1944 when the glass case in which the mummy was housed was shattered by bomb damage.

The lips, now as then, are parted and the tongue protrudes some 2 cm beyond the teeth. It was originally described as thin and flattened and still has that appearance (Fig. 52). During the present examination, there appeared to be some glue on the surface of the tongue. At first it was thought that this indicated restoration work on the tongue and that the latter had possibly been broken off along with the nose in 1944. However, Teale and Hey also noticed glue-like material on some organs including the tongue and it may well be that this does not represent modern restoration at all. It is interesting to speculate that the tongue broke off during the latter part of the mummification process but before it was wrapped and that the repair originates from that time.

The next question to consider is why the tongue protrudes from the mouth. A common reason for this would be that it was larger than normal. This could be due to cancers in the tongue or inflammation, but histological examination of the tongue shows no such abnormalities. Another possibility is that the tongue had swollen due to the accumulation of fluid in it, a condition known as oedema; this would not be detected histologically in mummified tissue, as this very process will have extracted the fluid from the tissue. Oedema of the tongue is usually the result of an allergic reaction. This may be part of a generalized response by the body following the consumption of an allergen such as a drug. More commonly, however, it occurs as a local reaction to an irritant coming into contact with the tongue, bee and wasp stings being the commonest cause. Both systemic and local reactions lead to death by choking.

Perhaps more sinister is the possibility that this man was strangled; certainly death from hanging, strangulation by ligature or by manual strangulation may be associated with protrusions of the tongue. There are no marks on the neck to suggest hanging or ligature strangulation but manual strangulation which may leave minimal marks on the neck cannot be excluded.

The only other known example of a protruding tongue in an Egyptian mummy is in the Petrie Museum at University College London. The cause in this case is also unknown.

Originally the mouth had been observed by Teale and Hey (1828) to be full of a powdered vegetable material and in our re-examination there was still a good deal of this material in the back of the mouth and throat. In view of the abnormalities of the tongue and the possibility of injury to the larynx during strangulation, it was particularly important that the attachment of the tongue at the back of the throat and the larynx below this should be examined. With this in mind as much as possible of the vegetable material was removed from the back of the mouth and throat with forceps and the remainder sucked out with a vacuum cleaner (Fig. 53). A good view down the throat could then be obtained with the endoscope and a thorough examination of this area was carried out (Fig. 54). No evidence of abnormalities in the back of the tongue or injury to the larynx could be seen. In addition, a small hole was made in the front of the neck just below the larynx and an endoscope introduced through this into the trachea. This enabled examination of the larynx from below; its normality was confirmed (Fig. 55).

It was noted at the original examination that the eyes appeared to have sunk into their sockets but did not seem to have been extracted and this is the condition in which the present workers found them. There was no evidence of attempts to simulate the eye with an iris drawn on a linen package or with the more sophisticated prosthesis fashioned from stone described by Sandison (1986). Interestingly, Sandison also remarks on the use of small onions as prostheses in the eye sockets of Ramesses IV.

The presence of the eyes was confirmed in the present mummy. By using an approach both from within the cranial cavity and from the face it was possible to extract the eyes intact, together with the contents of the orbit and the eyelids. The optic nerve which takes information concerning sight from the retina of the eye to the brain was also preserved by this

Fig. 53 (below left) *Vegetable material being removed with forceps from the back of Natsef-Amun's throat so that an endoscope can be passed down it to examine the back of the tongue*

Fig. 54 (below right) *A video camera records the views obtained by the endoscope as it is passed down the throat*

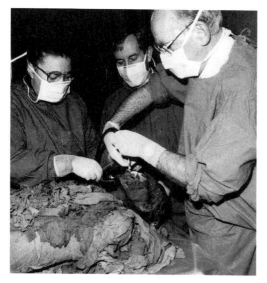

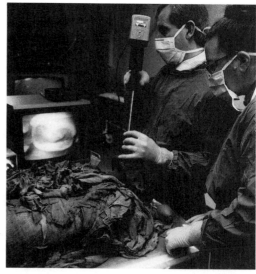

technique. The optic nerve is quite different from other cranial nerves in that it consists essentially of an extension of the brain tissue to the eye. Consequently under the microscope it has a distinctive structure which could be identified readily in the histological sections from the optic nerve of Natsef-Amun. This is in marked contrast to the only other histological examination of an optic nerve, reported by Ruffer (1911) who examined some sand-buried bodies of the Greek Period. The eyeballs could not be recognized in these cases and the microscopic structure of the optic nerves was greatly altered by the presence of moulds.

Whole sections of the eyeball were prepared in the present instance and the various parts such as the retina at the back of the eye and the cornea at the front could be seen. Between these the lens and the ciliary body were readily identified. The melanin pigment in the retina was particularly well preserved, a finding in keeping with that of Sandison (1986), the only other worker to have examined the eyes of Egyptian mummies in recent times.

Diseases of the eye are believed to have been common in ancient Egypt and in particular trachoma, caused by a virus-like organism, *Chlamydia trachomatous*, was probably a major cause of conjunctivitis and ultimately blindness. The disease is still common in Egypt and North Africa. Some worm infestations may also affect the eye and of these, filariasis is of particular interest, as it will be seen later that there was evidence of this disease elsewhere in the body. However, no evidence of filariasis could be seen in the present material from the eye and no other diseases of the eyeball were detected.

In addition to the eyeball and optic nerve, the orbit also contains muscles which control the eye movements and their accompanying nerves. Histological sections of one of the larger nerves supplying these muscles was examined and the degree of preservation of this nerve was quite remarkable. A wide range of stains was used to demonstrate both the axons and their myelin sheath. In some parts the myelin sheath appeared to be disrupted and the axons fragmented. Whilst it is not possible to be dogmatic about this, the appearances certainly suggest degeneration of the nerve fibres of the type found in a peripheral neuritis. This condition may occur in association with several metabolic diseases such as diabetes mellitus. It may also occur as a result of vitamin deficiency and in particular from a lack of vitamin B, a condition known as dry beri-beri. However, there is little evidence in the literature of this disease in ancient Egypt. Poisons and in particular some heavy metals such as lead may result in severe peripheral neuritis. Such substances were used therapeutically in ancient Egypt: possibly the treatment of

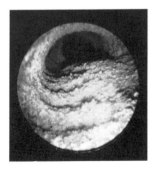

Fig. 55 *This is the view looking upwards through an endoscope in the trachea. In this way the larynx was examined and its structure seen to be intact*

the worm infestation suffered by Natsef-Amun could have resulted in his peripheral neuritis.

The skull had been opened in 1828 by removing part of the occipital bone at the back of the head (Fig. 56). At that time the skull was thick and remarkably firm. The membrane lining the skull was in its normal position and was preserved. There were a few lumps of resinous matter in the cavity but brain tissue could not be detected. After removing some of the resinous material, an opening in the base of the skull which communicated with the right nostril was identified and this was clearly the passage through which the embalmers had removed the brain. These findings were confirmed in the present examination. Samples of residual material from the base of the skull were examined under the microscope but this did not reveal any recognizable brain tissue and it is clear that the removal of the brain was remarkably complete in this instance.

The bandages on the front of the trunk had been replaced loosely following the original examination; when these were removed by the present workers it was seen that the chest wall was intact but much of the abdominal wall was missing (Fig. 57). In the earlier examination an embalming incision had been found on the left side of the abdomen extending 'from the cartilages of the ribs to the crest of the ilium'. The edges of this incision were almost intact but had not been sutured. Clearly this had been disturbed during Teale's examination of the abdomen and chest and in fact fragments of the abdominal wall were found in the loose packing which filled the cavity of the abdomen.

Since the present workers were uncertain as to the contents of the chest, it was decided to explore the chest cavity in the first place with the endoscope. As the anterior part of the chest was empty, it was possible to introduce an endoscope through the chest wall and check for the presence of residual organs or indeed the packages which were known to have been present in 1828 (Fig. 58). This examination being negative, the filling was then removed from the abdominal cavity and a thorough search was made for organs or packages. Fragments of tissue including parts of ribs were found in the packing but the examination confirmed Teale's observation that all the organs including the liver, stomach, intestines and kidneys had been removed from the abdomen. It was also possible to confirm that much of the diaphragm (the thin layer of muscle separating the abdominal and chest cavities) had been removed by the embalmers. Once the abdominal packing had been removed, the absence of the diaphragm allowed the chest cavity to be viewed directly. After removing some loose packing, the endoscopic findings in the chest could be confirmed and it was clear that the packages removed in 1828 had not been replaced.

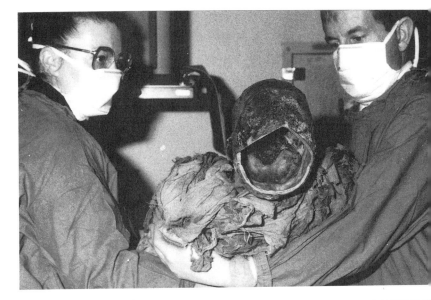

Fig. 56 *This opening in the back of the skull was made by the workers in 1828 so that they could examine the membranes lining the skull and check whether there was any residual brain tissue*

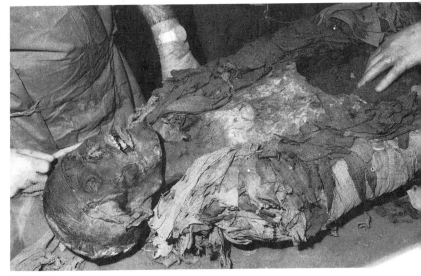

Fig. 57 *The chest wall of Natsef-Amun can be seen to be intact, but below this much of the abdominal wall is missing, the latter having been removed at the original examination in 1828*

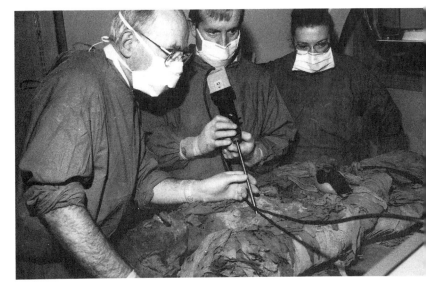

Fig. 58 *An endoscope has been introduced through the chest wall to see whether or not the packages which had been observed to be there at the original examination had been replaced*

Teale and Hey (1828) described the packages they found in the left side of the chest and drawings of these are illustrated in their report. They were certain from their shape that two of the packages were the kidneys although usually these are not removed during mummification. Another package was more irregular in outline and measured 6 × 2 in. (15 × 5 cm). It was described as having somewhat of a horseshoe figure. They noted a deep depression in the middle of this specimen, which they believed was due to a bandage having been firmly bound round this part whilst the organ was still soft. However, if the organs were wrapped after drying, as is now thought to be the case, it is unlikely that this is the explanation. If this organ was the liver as Teale and Hay believed, a more likely explanation for the groove would be that it is the one produced naturally in the liver by the backbone; in fact, its presence supports the suggestion that the organ was indeed the liver. One further package was thought by Teale and Hey to contain the heart. As these packages are not available for histological examination it is impossible to determine their true nature and unfortunately any disease they might have shown cannot be explored further.

Behind the loose packing in the chest there was some solid material which looked to the naked eye rather like cement. This was not commented on in the earlier report but, as it is extremely unlikely that the previous workers had introduced it, it

Fig. 59 *A photograph taken through a microscope to show a worm in tissue taken from the groin. The appearance of this worm indicates that it is of the filarial species. These worms block the lymphatic channels of the body which results in swelling of the groins and legs*

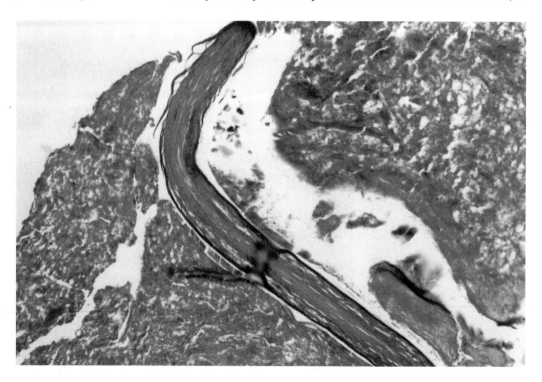

must be assumed that it was present at the time of their examination. Radiologically the material was opaque. It has been suggested that it must have been at least partly semi-liquid when it was introduced as there was a fluid level which was concave anteriorly, a finding compatible with compression by the insertion of the packing material before it had solidified. It is possible, however, that the hollows in this material were occupied by the packages removed by Teale and Hey in 1828. An analysis of this material is being carried out but its appearance suggests that it is largely natron.

The bandages had been removed from the front of the pelvis and groins during examination in 1828. It was not possible to recognize the penis but some irregular material which was thought to be the scrotum was submitted for histological examination. The sections consisted of skin, underlying fibrous tissue and fat. In several sections parts of a parasite could be identified and there is little doubt that this belongs to the group of worms known as the Filaria (Fig. 59). The adult worms are found in the lymphatic channels of the body and are viviparous, i.e. they give birth to larvae and do not lay eggs. These larvae are known as microfilaria and circulate in the blood, particularly at night, reaching their maximum numbers in the blood about midnight. These forms are not able to develop further unless they are ingested in blood by a mosquito. They then develop in the gut of the mosquito and reach the mouth area after about ten days. When the mosquito next sucks blood, infection of the human occurs and these forms are able to develop into adults found within the lymphatics.

The disease which is produced is known as filariasis. As the worm tends to block the lymphatic channels it produces fluid retention (oedema) in the parts drained by the lymphatics. Those in the groin tend to be affected most commonly and when the lymphatics in this area are blocked swelling of the legs, scrotum and vulva develops and may reach enormous proportions. This gross oedema is known as elephantiasis (Fig. 60). It can cause such enlargement of the scrotum that the sufferer has to support his scrotum in a wheelbarrow which he is obliged to push along in front of him (Fig. 61).

It is not possible to say just how severe the changes were in the case of Natsef-Amun since, as with other forms of oedema, the changes are obscured by mummification. There do not appear to be previous reports of this parasite being found in Egyptian mummies but, in view of the striking appearance of the disease, it would not be surprising if tomb paintings showing swelling of the legs were depictions of this disease. The Queen of Punt is illustrated as having grossly swollen legs and this has been described by some workers as dropsy. This is the term

Figs. 60 and 61 *Typical swellings of the groins* (above) *and scrotum* (below) *induced by the blockage of the lymphatics by filarial worms*

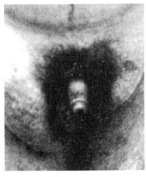

usually used when oedema of the legs due to heart failure is being described. However, isolated oedema of the legs and lower abdomen as depicted in the Queen of Punt could well be due to filariasis rather than to heart failure.

Evidence of a quite different disease was found when the femoral blood vessels from the groin were examined under the microscope, the femoral artery showing well-developed plaques of atheroma. This is a degenerative disease of the blood vessels which may result in the lumen being severely narrowed or even occluded. When this occurs the blood supply to that part of the body is cut off and this may result in strokes when vessels to the brain are affected or heart attacks when the coronary arteries are narrowed. In the present instance, progression of the disease could have resulted in Natsef-Amun suffering from severe cramps in the legs and ultimately gangrene of the feet.

Atherosclerosis has been reported previously in Egyptian mummies by Sandison (1962) and indeed, reference has already been made in the previous chapter to Shattock's examination of the aorta of the Pharaoh Menephtah. However, atherosclerosis was probably not the scourge in ancient Egypt that it is today. Two factors are probably responsible for this. In the first place, the diet of the ancient Egyptians did not contain the high levels of cholesterol and saturated fats which are present in modern foods. In addition, atherosclerosis is a progressive disease which tends to occur in middle life or later and the ancient Egyptians may well not have lived long enough to develop pathological levels of atheroma in their arteries.

During the course of the present chapter the methods of obtaining specimens of mummified tissue for histological examination have been outlined. Clearly 'biopsies' of the skin and subcutaneous tissue in intact mummies may reveal evidence of disease. Canopic jars and organs left within mummy wrappings are invaluable sources of material and have produced evidence of liver fluke infestations in a liver and strongyloides in some intestines. Post-mortem examination of the Two Brothers in the early part of this century did not reveal evidence of disease but the application of modern histological techniques have made it possible to show that Nekht-Ankh suffered from sand pneumoconiosis. More recently the autopsy in Mummy 1770 demonstrated that she suffered from Guinea worm infestation.

The development of endoscopic techniques has expanded the material available for study and shown evidence of hydatid disease in the brain of one mummy and in the lung of another. It has also shown that sand pneumoconiosis was probably a common disease in ancient Egypt.

The opportunity to study the Leeds Mummy has allowed a combination of endoscopic and autopsy techniques to be explored. The use of the endoscope to examine the neck of Natsef-Amun has been particularly valuable in allowing the throat and larynx to be visualized directly and examined for evidence of injury or disease without damaging the external appearance of the face or neck. These findings have been useful in attempts to determine the reason for the protrusion of the tongue. They show that there was no evidence that this was a manifestation of manual strangulation and indicate that it is unlikely that the protrusion of the tongue was due to a tumour in the back of the throat. The latter was confirmed by histological examination of the tongue.

Histological examination of the tissues has allowed reassessment of some of the findings described in the 1828 report. In particular, the demonstration under the microscope of adipoceferous crystals has confirmed the original workers' belief that the waxy appearance of the tissues was due to adipocere formation and not due to impregnation of the mummy by wax during the embalming process. Examination of the skin under the microscope showed that whilst the method of embalming had not preserved the epidermis, the underlying tissues had not had their staining characteristics altered in the manner which has been described in some mummies.

Removal of the eye complete with optic nerve and the contents of the orbit allowed histological examination of these structures. There was excellent preservation of the eyes and optic nerve; moreover, sections of the nerves supplying the muscles attached to the eye indicated that Natsef-Amun may have suffered from peripheral neuritis.

The absence of the packages from the mummy was disappointing, as these might have revealed evidence of disease. However, histological examination of tissues from the groin demonstrated that Natsef-Amun suffered from filariasis and might well have had a grossly enlarged scrotum and marked swelling of the legs. Furthermore, examination of the femoral arteries from the legs show well-developed plaques of atheroma which probably had not resulted in any disability by the time Natsef-Amun died but certainly could have led to gangrene if the condition had progressed.

12   Blood Grouping

T. Haigh and
T.A. Flaherty

Unlike dental and radiological investigations, the elucidation of blood groups in ancient mummies gives us no immediate insight into the everyday lives of these people. However, there are well-known associations between certain blood groups and disease states which allow us to infer the diseases to which certain mummies may have been prone. Blood groups have also been used to determine kinships and to follow geographical migrations. It must be stressed that testing for blood groups in mummified material intrinsically is extremely difficult; any subsequent information gained from the blood groups is secondary to the knowledge acquired in actually developing and applying the tests.

The discovery of blood groups

William Harvey's description of the circulatory system published in *De Motu Cordis* (1628) provoked interest in the possibility of transfusing blood between different individuals. Several instances of the technique were reported during the next eighty years or so. Early experiments also concerned the transfusion of chemicals such as beer, water and even dilute acid solutions into animals. A blood transfusion between two dogs was reported in 1665. Over the next few years the transfusion of blood from animals to man was attempted but, following legal problems concerning the death of a multiply transfused individual in Paris, the practice was banned in both France and Britain and fell into disuse for more than a hundred years.

James Blundell, a physician working in London, next recognized its potential as a treatment for circulatory collapse associated with severe bleeding that sometimes occurs with childbirth. He realized the dangers inherent in animal to man transfusions and recommended the use of human blood and then only in an emergency. Throughout the nineteenth century many attempts were made to overcome problems and to improve techniques. One aspect which caused difficulty was the fact that the blood clotted if it remained outside the body for any length of time. Various experiments were carried out to prevent this by adding different substances to the blood. Today mixtures of dextrose and citrate are found to be the most effective in preventing blood clotting and this is one of the reasons why blood can now be stored in a fridge for four to six weeks after donation.

It has been recognized for many years that not all blood was suitable for transfusion from one individual to another. If the blood was incompatible, the person receiving the blood reacted to it in such a way that the red cells of their own blood stuck together (agglutinated); and this usually resulted in severe kidney damage which in many cases caused the death of the recipient. The incompatibility problem was not really solved until the first years of the twentieth century when Landsteiner, Sturli and De Castello showed that the serum, i.e. the liquid part of the blood, from one individual, when mixed with red blood cells of other individuals, reacted with some of the cells but not with others. Based on these observations, Landsteiner reported three blood groups which he named A, B and O and indicated their potential importance in relation to the successful practice of blood transfusion. Soon afterwards other workers reported the existence of a fourth blood group which they named AB. Since then more than 200 blood group antigens have been discovered, including the M, N and P systems and the very important Rhesus system. Generally speaking in current blood transfusion practice it is only necessary to determine the ABO and Rhesus group of donor and recipient to provide compatible blood.

Blood groups

Because of the way the body's immune system is regulated, antigens present on cells are not usually accompanied by a corresponding antibody. Sometimes this well-ordered state breaks down and an individual may develop antibodies against his own tissues, e.g. thyroid or kidney, and then suffers from what is called an autoimmune disease. Blood groups obey similar rules so that the presence of an A antigen on the red cell is accompanied by an antibody in the serum which has anti-B activity. The antigens and antibodies of the ABO system together with some examples of frequency and distribution are shown in Tables 1 and 2.

Table 1

Antigens and antibodies of ABO system

Blood group	O	A	B	AB
Antigen on red cells	none	A	B	A & B
Serum antibody	anti-A anti-B	anti-B	anti-A	none

Table 2

Frequency of blood groups in various countries

Group	UK %	North India %	South India %	Egypt %
O	52	38	47	36
A	37	38	19	33
B	8	19	26	24
AB	3	3	6	7

The nature and distribution of ABO antigens in human tissues

AB and O antigens are relatively simple in structure mostly made up of long chains of sugar molecules (polysaccharides). A and B antigens differ only in having a different sugar molecule at the end of the chain. The O 'antigen' is a slightly more primitive polysaccharide which lacks the ability to produce A or B determinants and is therefore classified as O.

The relative simplicity of these molecules is important in the context of determining blood groups of mummified tissues. It is easy to conceive that they could be lost or altered in some way which could give rise to a false result; contamination with bacterial products, plant material or various herbs and spices such as might have been used in the embalming process and which themselves are rich in sugars could give misleading results.

Blood group antigens of the ABO system are not confined to red cell membranes but are found in most tissues of the body. In dealing with mummies, the most readily available are muscle, bone and skin as it is very rare to find intact red blood cells in a sufficient state of preservation to give reliable results.

Inheritance of the ABO system

ABO groups are inherited in the classic Mendelian fashion. In its simplest form each parent has two genes (genotype) which govern the expression of the blood group (phenotype). One or other of these genes is passed on by each parent to its offspring. A and B genes are dominant and take precedence over O so that an individual will be group A whether the A gene is present in double (AA) or single dose (AO). A summary of the gene combinations that produce each blood group is given in Table 3.

Table 3

Genotypes and phenotypes of ABO blood groups

Genotype	Phenotype/Blood Group
OO	Group O
AA	Group A
AO	
BB	Group B
BO	
AB	Group AB

Table 4

Influence of parents' blood on child's blood group

Parents' blood group	A : A	A : A	AB : AB
Parents' genotype	AA × AA	AO × AO	AB × AB
Child's genotype	AA AA AA AA	AA AO OA OO	AA AB BA BB
Child's blood group	A A A A	A A A O	A AB AB B

It has been mentioned already that blood groups may be of use in establishing relationships between different mummies. However, it can be seen from looking at Table 4, that an offspring's blood group does not necessarily have to be the same as its parents. Although blood groups are used in present-day testing for proof of paternity the procedure is quite complicated and involves much more than just a simple ABO grouping. Given that ABO grouping is usually all that is available from mummies, it is unlikely that positive proof of relationship could be established using this system alone. DNA fingerprinting is likely to be much more relevant in this context.

The study of blood groups in mummified tissues

Less than thirty years were to elapse between the definition of the four ABO blood groups and the first reported attempt at blood grouping in ancient tissues. In 1929 the Katsunamas attempted the typing of neolithic remains from Shell Mounds in Japan and some years later in the 1930s the Boyds, Candela and Matson in separate studies also attempted to determine the blood groups of ancient tissues. All these workers tended to use the same method which was the absorption inhibition test. This test relies on the fact that if appropriately prepared tissue is exposed to a serum containing a blood group antibody, e.g. anti-A, and the serum is subsequently found to contain less anti-A than before, then it can be assumed that the blood group antigen A is present in the tissue and has absorbed the antibody.

This test is quite straightforward in theory but in practice is fraught with difficulties. Apart from the problems of producing a suitable tissue preparation, the specific antisera available in the 1930s were relatively uncontrolled and varied both in avidity and titre. In interpreting the published results the shortcomings of the grouping reagents and factors such as the age of the tissue, the conditions of storage subsequent to exhumation and various known and unknown contaminants have all to be borne in mind. It is possible that early studies produced false results. Tissues may have been grouped as A or B or AB because of nonspecific absorption of the antibody by factors other than the relevant blood group antigens. If no absorption occurred, perhaps because the blood group antigens had deteriorated, then the tissue would be falsely grouped as Group O. This can be seen in Table 5, where separate studies of the same specimens by different people produced quite marked differences in the results.

Table 5

Results of blood grouping of the same specimens by different workers

Blood Group	O	A	B	AB
Boyd	30	0	0	0
Candela	11	11	6	2
Lippold	10	14	3	1

More recent workers using newer techniques have also encountered the problem of reliability and validity of results. In 1975 Lengyel described a fluorescent antibody technique used on over 5000 samples of bones from Hungarian cemeteries. The bones ranged in origin from the prehistoric times to the early Middle Ages. Only one-third of the material tested was classed as being fully suitable for evaluation. Lengyel once again noted probable effects of decomposition occurring between death and burial and during and after burial and excavation. He also mentions modification or loss of antigen activity due to bacterial enzymes. Bacteria are very common and many are capable of producing substances similar to A and B antigens (Table 6).

Table 6
Bacteria producing blood group-like substances

E. Coli	B
Toxicara	A/B
Shigella	A/B/H(O)
Clostridia	A/B

Plant material which may easily contaminate the tissues causes problems because of the variety of the antibody-like substances they produce (Table 7). Although none of Lengyel's specimens was from a mummy, the reservations expressed about the technique and the conditions of the testing apply with even greater force to mummified tissue.

Table 7
Plant substances having antibody activity against ABO groups

Lectin	*Specificity*
Dolichos biflorus	Anti-A
Ulex europaeus	Anti-H(O)
Crotalaria	Anti-A & B

The influence of biotechnology on the problem of blood grouping

Monoclonal antibodies: Efforts have been made down the years to provide ever more reliable and effective reagents for blood group testing. It was not until the 1950s that any degree of standardization was applied to their production and in the last ten years very specific reagents have resulted from the development of monoclonal antibodies. There are produced by fusing together two cells, one of which is capable of producing the requisite antibody and the other, usually a cancer cell, has the ability to reproduce itself independently. This fusion results in a cellular factory which produces particular and highly specific antibody almost indefinitely. The use of these reagents in mummies has shown considerable promise but problems still arise from the handling and preparation of the tissues.

Genetic fingerprinting: This was first developed by Jeffreys at Leicester University and has recently been applied to mummified tissues. The principle of the test is that the genetic information for all individuals is made up of deoxyribonucleic acid (DNA). By the use of various enzymes and radiological techniques the DNA in the cells can be broken up to give a unique pattern for each individual. The results look something like a supermarket bar code and allow for relatively easy comparison between individuals. The technique is used quite extensively in paternity testing and in forensic medicine. An identical pattern between two samples would be taken to imply that they both came from the same individual or from identical twins. DNA fingerprinting has nothing to do with blood group but could prove very valuable in determining kinships between mummies.

HLA antigens: These are tissue antigens separate from blood groups and are involved with immune responses. They are important in current medical practice as compatibility between these antigens in the donor and recipient is necessary for successful organ transplantation. Attempts have been made to use this system on mummified tissue and Stastny has reported success in HLA typing of mummified Peruvian remains.

Particular HLA antigens are associated with diseases such as diabetes. Again these linkages could be informative regarding disease states in ancient civilizations.

Blood grouping of mummies in Preston

During the last ten years, work in Preston on the mummy from the Manchester Museum has centred on the investigation and application of the various techniques described by the earlier workers. It was hoped that the improvements in the ABO blood grouping reagents which were then becoming more readily available would give more reliable results. Initially the techniques had to be mastered using fresh tissue which was available from post-mortem specimens. These results were quite promising but working with mummified tissue was much more difficult. As monoclonal antibodies became available they were also incorporated into the battery of tests. Table 8 shows the results of exposing selected mummy tissues to blood group antisera containing anti-A & B. After incubation the sera are tested for what remains and from that it can be deduced which antibody has been absorbed. It can be seen that both antibodies have been absorbed in the first four mummies tested which therefore seem to be group AB but the serum tested after incubation with Mummy 21474 reacts with anti-A alone suggesting that only anti-B has been taken up and this tissue can be presumed to be group B.

While these newer techniques and reagents have undoubtedly helped, the possibility that the blood group antigens become altered during the tissue extraction remains a problem and because of that the complete reliability of the results must be in doubt. The state of the tissues varies greatly from sample to sample and it is difficult to achieve a foolproof and reproducible method of handling and extraction. Each tissue must be degraded on an individually controlled basis and the digestion of tissue using various enzymes is also somewhat problematical.

Table 8
The use of specific monocloanl antibodies

Mummy

21475	Anti A & B	–	21476	Anti A & B	–
7740	Anti A & B	–	21474	Anti A	+++
				Anti B	–
5275	Anti A & B	–			

The experience gained in this work has recently been applied to extracting a suitable preparation from a rib of the Leeds mummy, Natsef-Amun. This material, though stored in an uncontrolled manner for many years, should, in theory at least, be a good source of blood group antigens. The tissue has been subjected to aqueous and alcoholic extraction processes and the cellular content has been solubilized in detergents. Portions have also been selectively degraded using various enzymes in different dilutions. All tissue extracts have been tested by a monoclonal antibody technique. All the samples tested have failed to react when tested with anti-A and anti-B and the tissue may therefore tentatively presumed to be Group O.

Further work remains to be done to verify the results and also to render the present technique as reliable as possible. Standardized preparation of the test material remains a challenge and because of this there is always the danger that a negative result with both reagents represents nonreactive tissue or conversely a positive result with both reagents may represent nonspecificity. Tests need to be developed to ensure freedom from false results due to bacterial contamination of the material and some technique is required to estimate quality of the tissues before the examination is undertaken.

It is likely that genetic fingerprinting will eventually be applied successfully to mummified tissue in the elucidation of kinships, and a reliable routine test for blood group antigens could provide information about disease states and about other factors which make continued attempts to find a suitable method worthwhile.

13 The Facial Reconstruction of Natsef-Amun

R.A.H. Neave

The occupants of the Natufian encampment at Tel-es-Sultan, Jericho (c.700 BC) deposited the heads of their dead separately from the rest of their bodies. This practice was not uncommon in Mesolithic times. The unique factor about the examples found at this site (excavated by Kenyon in 1953) is the manner in which the features of the faces have been delicately built in plaster on to the skulls, giving an impression of artistic skills in portraiture far more sophisticated than could be expected from that period.

The basic concept of the underlying bony structure influencing the outward appearance of a living creature is well understood and acknowledged by both scientist and artist. Indeed, it was Galen who, in his book *De Anatomicis Administrationibus*, written c.AD 130, observed 'as poles to tents and walls to houses so are bones to living creatures, for other features naturally take from them and change with them'. Thus, while the Tel-es-Sultan specimens cannot necessarily be seen as reconstructions of the deceased's face, it is quite likely that they do give some indication of how those people would have looked in life.

Of course, there have been occasions when the bones of very ancient animals have given rise to some conflicting interpretations, none more so than in the study of *Homo sapiens*. For many years anthropologists and anatomists have been attempting to discover exactly how our early ancestor looked in life.

One of the earliest and most frequently quoted experiments undertaken in an attempt to reconstruct the appearance of the face and head of early Stone Age man was that of a Swiss scientist, Kollmann, and the sculptor Büchly (Kollmann and Büchly, 1898). Theirs was the first truly scientific reconstruction. Kollmann prepared a series of tables which listed the average thickness of soft tissue at twenty-three points on the face. These measurements were combined with a similar set of figures prepared by the anatomist His, and, until recently, have served as the only measurements of their kind; then, as now, the technique consisted of building the soft tissue on to the skull. Using clay or some similar 'plastic' material, the features were developed, ensuring that the thickness of the tissue conformed to the prescribed measurements.

Anatomists and anthropologists produced many further attempts using similar methods. In 1910, the anatomist Solger constructed the head of Neanderthal man, using a youth of the same type as the starting point. Three years later, Professor Eggeling of Jena University constructed the head of another Neanderthal man and, at the same time, the anthropologist Martin was undertaking the same task, using a cast of the same skull; the results, however, were quite different. A favourite skull, used for many reconstructions, was the La Chapelle-aux-Saints specimen, but the results all differed widely and the idea that an accurate reconstruction was possible came to be regarded with grave suspicion. Despite these misgivings, there remained a strong belief amongst anatomists that an unmistakable correlation existed between the living face and the skull.

One of these anatomists, Welked, identified Raphael's skull by comparing it with the artist's self-portraits. Later, the anatomist Geiss identified the remains of Bach, Kant and Haydn, using the skull portrait technique. An experiment undertaken in 1908 by the sculptor Sefner, who tried to reproduce the head of the composer Handel on the skull of composer Bach, demonstrated how it was necessary to abandon all the laws of normal anatomy to achieve the desired result. It was not until 1913 that Professor Eggeling of Jena University designed an experiment by which he hoped to prove finally the accuracy of the skull–head reconstruction technique.

First, he cast the head of a recently deceased man, then he measured the soft tissue at specific points. Having removed the soft tissue, he prepared two plaster casts of the skull and gave them, together with the relevant information, to two separate sculptors who, working independently of each other, were to recreate the face. The results were not as expected, for not only were the two reproductions unlike each other, but they were also both quite unlike the original. It is obvious to us today

The reconstructed heads of the Two Brothers.

Fig. 62
(above)*Nekht-Ankh*

Fig. 63 (below)
Khnum-Nakht compared with his tomb statuette,
Fig. 64 (bottom)

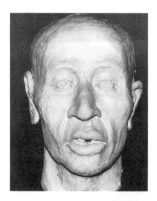

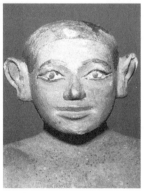

that neither sculptor worked as accurately as necessary and also that both had allowed their own free expression to override what is basically a technical exercise.

Despite the very considerable amount of work that was done by the anatomists, sculptors and anthropologists in the late nineteenth and early twentieth centuries, relatively little effort was put into developing an ordered system whereby their methods could be developed and explored in a methodical manner, and their validity or otherwise rested on one or two isolated experiments, instead of on a series of carefully controlled tests. A notable exception was Professor Mikhail Gerasimov who, until his death in 1970, was the Director of the Laboratory of Plastic Reconstruction at the Ethnographical Institute of the USSR in Moscow. His work was confined mostly to the faces of palaeolithic man and historical figures, but forensic reconstructions, about a hundred in all, did give him the opportunity to test his work 'in the field', and the results proved that his methods and techniques were indeed credible.

This brief résumé cannot cover every event or aspect in the work of facial reconstruction that has taken place or is currently being pursued. It is included primarily to show that such work is neither revolutionary nor unscientific, and like many arcane subjects, it embraces workers from many different backgrounds and cannot be considered as being in the mainstream of science.

Such work was not undertaken at Manchester University until 1973 when the faces of two ancient Egyptian brothers were reconstructed, and the results, while rather crude, were nevertheless of some value (Figs. 62, 63, 64). In 1975, the head of a third ancient Egyptian, Mummy 1770, was reconstructed (Fig. 65), and the rebuilding of this third head triggered a chain of events that led into other periods of archaeological study and into forensic science, as with the example of Phillip II of Macedon. Despite the obvious limitations and difficulties confronted when undertaking such an exercise, it has become clear that a reconstruction, if carried out in the correct manner, will always have a very close resemblance to the individual as he or she was in life.

When any facial reconstruction is being planned, the first prerequisite is to have access to the skull, or a cast of the skull. Until relatively recently, the only way this could be achieved in the case of embalmed (mummified) subjects was physically to remove the skull. Standard radiographs can now enable a model of the skull to be prepared (David, 1986; Stead et al, 1986). This technique relies naturally upon the suitability of the radiographs, it is labour-intensive, and it can be subject to dimensional inaccuracy. To develop the techniques of non-invasive study of ancient Egyptian mummies further, the body of the Leeds

Fig. 65 *The reconstructed head of Mummy 1770*

Figs. 66, 67, 68 *A three-dimensional image of the skull of Natsef-Amun, as displayed on the computer*

Mummy, Natsef-Amun, was examined using x-ray computer tomography. This provides information upon the varying densities of different materials and structures within the body of the mummy which is held in digital form on magnetic tape. This work was carried out in the Department of Diagnostic Radiology at the University of Manchester.

The information on tape was next taken to the Department of Medical Physics and Bio-Engineering at University College Hospital, London, where Dr A. Linney transferred the digital information on to a computer screen. By careful manipulation of the data, a three-dimensional image of the mummy's skull could be displayed (Figs. 66, 67, 68). The next stage was to produce a solid replica of the image upon which the face could be built. This was achieved by using a sophisticated numerically controlled milling machine which carved the replica from a block of polystyrene (Linney et al., 1991).

There was now available a dimensionally accurate model of the skull, the original of which remained undisturbed. It is hardly surprising that a good deal of the fine detail of the skull was not present on the model, but it was certainly very much more accurate than any of the previous techniques.

Despite obvious limitations and restraints, reconstruction of the soft tissues of the head and face on to a dry skull does in most cases give a very good idea of how an individual would have looked in life. Control studies on cadavers have demonstrated that a reconstruction is far less speculative than it may first appear to be. Practical work in the forensic field has provided numerous opportunities to compare reconstructions with photographs of the subjects when alive. Such work has also resulted in unidentified bodies being identified by either family or friends, and has sometimes resulted in the arrest and subsequent conviction of some of the assailants of these unfortunate individuals. It is, however, very important to understand that, whilst a strong similarity can be achieved, it is not possible

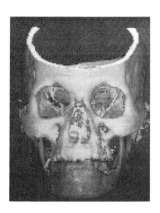
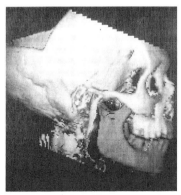
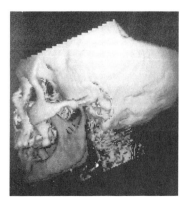

to produce a completely accurate portrait, since there are too many variables, both in terms of tissue thickness and in surface details such as spots, folds, wrinkles, creases, scars, and so forth. The exact details of the eyes cannot be gleaned from the skull alone, and neither can the shape of the lips, the tip of the nose or the ears; all these features are inevitably subject to experience and 'feel'. Thus, when we come to consider a reconstruction of the head of Natsef-Amun, it can be argued that certain details are not totally accurate, but his close friends and family would almost certainly recognize him.

The method of rebuilding the soft tissue is undertaken in a very specific manner and, whether the subject under consideration has been dead for three years or three thousand, the method is basically the same. Working upon the replica skull, twenty-one small wooden pegs project from the surface of the skull and represent the average thickness of soft tissue that can be found at those specific sites. These measurements, produced in 1983 (Rhine and Moore, 1983), give a range between emaciated and obese, male and female, but they are not specific to any particular ethnic group, being based on American Caucasians, and provide a basic groundsheet that can be employed to ensure consistency. Simulated eyeballs are fitted into position in the orbital cavities over which the eyelids will subsequently be modelled. The prepared skull is then mounted on a sturdy iron stand and the basic neck structure is blocked in, using modelling clay; the muscles of the face are built in position, starting with the major muscles of mastication, and moving on to those that surround the eyes, the mouth and the muscles of expression. This exercise is not an attempt to produce a highly detailed anatomical model, but to ensure that the head and face progress in an organized and controlled manner and grow from the surface of the skull outwards.

The rules governing the shape of the nose and the mouth are carefully observed, although great care has to be taken with these features. It was clear from the skull of Natsef-Amun that the nose would be broad and flat and that the lips would be full. The position and spatial distribution of the features of any face are of course determined by the bony structure of the skull, and the features will grow and develop automatically, provided that all the groundwork has been done correctly and that the work has adhered to the basic principles. In the case of Natsef-Amun, a face with somewhat negroid features emerged; he is shown as a man in his mid-forties with slight creasing of the forehead, and a shaven head as befits a priest of his period (Fig. 69). Of course, such creases must remain purely speculative and this is also the case with the exact detail of the eyes, the outline of the vermilion of the lips and the nasolabial fold; these may have been

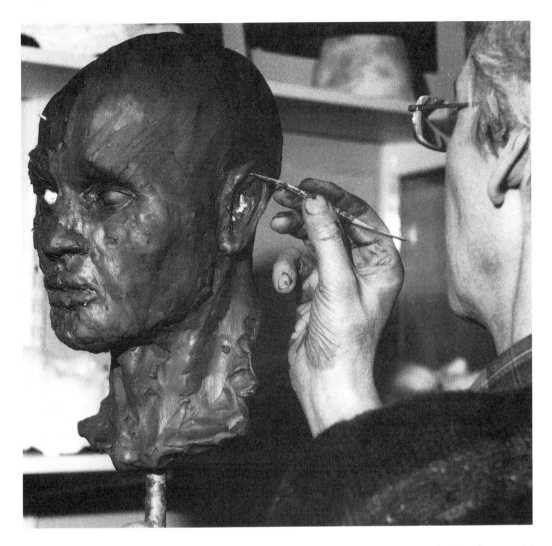

Fig. 69 *Richard Neave completes the reconstruction of the head of Natsef-Amun*

very much more clearly defined and it is unlikely that they would be less so in a man of his age, living in a hot, dry climate.

A reconstruction such as this endeavours to show the individual as he may have appeared in life; it is a synthesis of all the facts that have been established from detailed examination of the complete skeleton, the skull and teeth. In addition, the background of his lifestyle and occupation, as well as the historical period in which he lived, are taken into account.

It is not difficult to visualize this man living in the world of the pharaohs, with all its mystery and romance, and, indeed, such images can become so strong that reconstructions are sometimes regarded as something apart from the rest of a study. However, this is not the case, for they form but a small part of a much wider scientific study.

Chronological Table

Predynastic Period (c. 5000-c. 3100 BC)
  Unification of Egypt *c.* 3100 BC

Archaic Period (c. 3100-c. 2686 BC)
  1st and 2nd Dynasties

Old Kingdom (c. 2686-c. 2181 BC)
  3rd to 6th Dynasties

First Intermediate Period (c. 2181-c. 1991 BC)
  7th to 11th Dynasties

Middle Kingdom (1991–1786 BC)
  12th Dynasty

Second Intermediate Period (1786–1567 BC)
  13th to 17th Dynasties

New Kingdom (1567–1085 BC)
  18th to 20th Dynasties
  20th Dynasty 1200–1085 BC: Reign of Ramesses XI (1113–1085 BC) when Natsef-Amun lived at Thebes

Third Intermediate Period (c. 1089–525 BC)
  21st to 26th Dynasties

Late Period (525–332 BC)
  27th to 31st Dynasties
  Conquest of Egypt by Alexander the Great 332 BC, who ruled until his death in 323 BC

Ptolemaic Period (323–30 BC)
  Conquest of Egypt by Augustus (Octavian) 30 BC

Roman period 30 BC–AD 641
  Arab Conquest AD 641.

References

Chapter 1   Belzoni, G., *Narrative of the Operations and Recent Discoveries within the Pyramids, Temples, Tombs and Excavations in Egypt and Nubia* (London, 1821)

Edwards, A.B., *A Thousand Miles up the Nile* (London, 1877)

Fagan, B., *The Rape of the Nile* (London, 1975)

Granville, A.B., 'An Essay on Egyptian Mummies, with Observations on the Art of Embalming amongst Ancient Egyptians' in *Philosophical Transactions of the Royal Society* (1825), pp. 269–316

Lucas, A., *Ancient Egyptian Materials and Industries* (1926); 4th ed. rev. and enlarged by J.R. Harris (London, 1962)

Moodie, R.L., (ed.), *Studies in the Palaeopathology of Egypt* (Cairo, 1921)

Murray, M.A., *The Tomb of Two Brothers* (Manchester Museum Handbook, Manchester, 1910)

Parey, A., *The Works of that Famous Chirurgion Ambrose Parey* (London, 1634) in Pettigrew (1834), p. 448

Petrie, W.M., *Methods and Aims in Archaeology* (London, 1904)

Pettigrew, T.J., *A History of Egyptian Mummies and an Account of the Worship and Embalming of Sacred Animals* (London, 1834). Everyman's Library (London, 1964)

Smith, G.E., *The Royal Mummies* (Cairo, 1912)

Smith, G.E. and Dawson, W.R., *Egyptian Mummies* (London, 1924; rev. ed. 1991)

Chapter 3   Cockburn, A. and E. (eds.), *Mummies, Disease and Ancient Cultures* (Cambridge, 1980)

David, A.R., (ed.), *The Manchester Museum Mummy Project* (Manchester, 1979): Garner, R.C., 'Experimental Mummification', pp. 19–24

Dawson, W.R., 'Making a Mummy' in *Journal of Egyptian Archaeology*, Vol. 13 (1927), pp. 40–49 and plates xvii and xviii

Diodorus Siculus, *History, Book I*, para. 91 (transl. by C.H. Oldfather, Loeb Classical Library, Cambridge, Mass., 1968)

Glob, P.V., *The Bog People* (London, 1969)

Herodotus, *The Histories, Book II*, para. 86–88 (transl. by A.D. Godley, Loeb Classical Library, Cambridge, Mass., 1946)

Leek, F.F., 'The problem of brain removal during embalming by the ancient Egyptians' in *Journal of Egyptian Archaeology*, Vol. 55 (1969), pp. 112–116

Lucas, A., 'The use of natron by the ancient Egyptians in mummification' in *Journal of Egyptian Archaeology*, Vol. 1 (1914), pp. 119–158

Lucas, A., 'The use of natron in mummification' in *Journal of Egyptian Archaeology*, Vol. 18 (1932), pp. 125–140

Lucas, A., 'Artificial eyes in ancient Egypt' in *Ancient Egypt*, Vol. 2 (1934), pp. 84–99

Lucas, A., *Ancient Egyptian Materials and Industries* (1926); 4th ed. rev. and enlarged by J.R. Harris (London, 1962)

Sakurai, Kiyohiko and Ogata, Tamotsu, 'Japanese Mummies' in Cockburn and Cockburn (1980), pp. 211–223

Sandison, A.T., 'The use of natron in mummification in ancient Egypt' in *Journal of Near Eastern Studies*, Vol. 22 (1963), pp. 259 ff

Smith, G.E. and Dawson, W.R., *Egyptian Mummies* (London, 1924; rev. ed. 1991)

Chapter 4   Daressy, G., 'Contribution à l'étude de la XXIe dynasties' in *Revue Archéologique*, Janvier 1896

Daressy, G., 'Les Sépultures des Prêtres d'Ammon à Deir el Bahri' in *Annales du Service des Antiquités de l'Égypte*, Vol. 1 (1900), pp. 141–148

Daressy, G., 'Les Cercueils des Prêtres d'Ammon' in *Annales du Service des*

Antiquités de l'Égypte, Vol. 8 (1907), No. 152, pp. 14 and 38

Daressy, G., *Cercueils de Cachettes Royales* (Cairo, 1909)

Daressy, G. and Smith, G.E., 'Ouvertures des Momies provenant de la Seconde Trouvaille de Deir el Bahri' in *Annales du Service des Antiquités de l'Égypte*, Vol. 4 (1903), pp. 150–152, 156–157

Lucas, A., *Ancient Egyptian Materials and Industries* (1926); 4th ed. rev. and enlarged by J.R. Harris (London, 1962)

Maspero, G., 'Les momies royales de Deir el Bahri, 1889' in *Mémoires . . . de la Mission archéologique française au Caire*, Tome I

Osburn, W., *An Account of an Egyptian Mummy presented to the Museum of the Leeds Philosophical and Literary Society by the late John Blayds, Esq.* (Leeds, 1828)

Passalacqua, J., *Catalogue raisonné et historique des antiquités découvertes en Égypte*. 3 parts. (1826)

Pettigrew, T.J., *A History of Egyptian Mummies and an Account of the Worship and Embalming of Sacred Animals* (London, 1834). Everyman's Library (London, 1964)

Porter, B. and Moss, R.L.B., *Topographical Bibliography of Ancient Egyptian Hieroglyphic Texts, Reliefs and Paintings*, Vol. 1. *The Theban Necropolis*, Part 2: Royal Tombs and Smaller Cemeteries (2nd rev. ed., Oxford, 1989), p. 637

Smith, G.E., *The Royal Mummies* (Cairo, 1912)

Chapter 5 Černý, J.A., *A Community of Workmen at Thebes in the Ramesside Period* (Cairo, 1973)

Herodotus, *The Histories, Book II* (transl. by A.D. Godley, Loeb Classical Library, Cambridge, Mass., 1946)

Peet, T.E., *The Great Tomb Robberies of the Twentieth Egyptian Dynasty*. 2 Vols. (Oxford, 1930)

Chapter 6 Attick, R.D., *The Shows of London* (Cambridge, Mass, 1978)

Brears, P., 'Ralph Thoresby, a Museum Visitor in Stuart England' in *Journal of the History of Collections* Vol. 1, no. 2 (Oxford, 1989), p. 218

Brears, P. and Davies, S., *Treasures for the People* (Leeds, 1989)

Champollion, J.F., *Précis du Système Hiéroglyphique des Anciens Egyptiens* (Paris, 1824)

Fetherston, F.M., *Oops and Doons . . . of Timothy Goorkrodger* (Huddersfield, c.1870) p. 79

Osburn, W., I. Letter to J. Phillips dated 2/2/1828 in the archives of the Yorkshire Philosophical Society, York

Osburn, W., II. *An Account of an Egyptian Mummy presented to the Museum of the Leeds Philosophical and Literary Society* Leeds (1828)

Phillips, G.S., *The Transcendentalism of Leeds* (Leeds, 1849) p. 120

Slade and Roebuck, *Directory of Leeds* (Leeds, 1851)

Wortham, J.D., *British Egyptology* (Newton Abbot, 1971)

Chapter 7 David, A.R., (ed.), *Mysteries of the Mummies: the Story of the Manchester University Investigation* (London, 1978)

David, A.R., (ed.), *The Manchester Museum Mummy Project* (Manchester, 1979)

David, A.R., (ed.), *Science in Egyptology* (Manchester, 1986)

David, A.R. and Tapp, E., (eds.), *Evidence Embalmed* (Manchester, 1984)

Murray, M.A., *The Tomb of Two Brothers* (Manchester Museum Handbook, Manchester, 1910)

Chapter 8 Dawson, W.R. and Gray, P.H.K., *Catalogue of Egyptian Antiquities in the British Museum (1): Mummies and Human Remains* (Oxford University Press, 1968)

Elliot Smith, G., *The Royal Mummies*, Catalogue Général des Antiquités du Egyptiennes du Musée du Caire, No. 61051–61100 (Service des Antiquités de l'Egypte, Cairo, 1912), pp. iii–iv

Fawcitt, R.A., Jarvis, H., and Isherwood, I., 'X-Raying the Manchester Mummies' in A.R. David and E. Tapp, (eds.), *Evidence Embalmed*, (Manchester Univ. Press, 1984), pp. 45–64

Gray, P.H.K., 'Calcinosis Intervertebralis with Special Reference to Similar Changes found in Mummies of Ancient Egyptians' in D. Brothwell, A.T. Sandison, C.C. Thomas, (eds.), *Diseases of Antiquity*, (Illinois, 1967), pp. 20–30

Gray, P.H.K. and Slow, D., *Egyptian Mummies in the City of Liverpool Museums* (Liverpool Corporation, 1968)

Gray, P.H.K., 'Radiological Aspects of the Mummies of Ancient Egyptians in the Rijksmuseum van Oudheden, Leiden' Reprinted from *Oudheidkundige mededelingen uit het Rijksmuseum van Oudheden, Leiden*, p. 47, (Leiden, 1966)

Gray, P.H.K., 'Notes Concerning the Position of Arms and Hands of Mummies with a View to Possible Dating of the Specimen' in *Journal of Egyptian Archaeology*, Vol. 58 (1972) pp. 200–04

Holland, Thurstan, 'X-rays in 1896', *The Liverpool Medico-Chirurgical Journal*, Vol. 45, (1937), p. 61

Isherwood, I., Jarvis, H. and Fawcitt, R.A., 'Radiology of the Manchester Mummies' in A.R. David, (ed.), *The Manchester Museum Mummy Project* (Manchester, 1979), pp. 25–64

Isherwood, I., and Jarvis, H., 'The Radiological Examination' in A.R. David (ed.) *Mysteries of the Mummies*, (London, 1978) pp. 109–127

König, W., *14 photographien mit Rontgen-Strahlen, aufgenommen im Physikalischen Verein*, (J.A. Barth, Frankfurt a M., Leipzig, 1896)

Moodie, R.L., *Roentgenological Studies of Egyptian Peruvian Mummies* (Field Museum of Natural History, Chicago, Illinois, 1931)

Murray, M.A., *The Tomb of Two Brothers* (Manchester Museum Handbook, Manchester, 1910)

Petrie, W.M.F., *Deshashesh 1897, Fifteenth Memoir of the Egypt Exploration Fund* (Egypt Exploration Fund, London, 1898), plate xxxvii

Ruffer, M.A., 'Studies in Palaeopathology in Egypt' in *Journal of Path. and Bact.*, Vol. 18 (1913), p. 149

Sandison, A.T., 'Diseases of the Eye' in D. Brothwell, A.T. Sandison, C.C. Thomas, (eds.), *Diseases of Antiquity*, (Illinois, 1967), pp. 457–463

Sandison, A.T., 'The Egyptian Mummy Eye', in A.R. David, (ed.), *Science in Egyptology*, (Manchester, 1986), pp. 7–9

Chapter 9 Leek, F.F., 'Teeth and Bread in Ancient Egypt' in *Journal of Egyptian Archaeology*, Vol. 58 (1972), pp. 126–132

Pahl, W.M., 'The Ritual Opening of the Mouth: Arguments for an Actual-Body Ritual from the Viewpoint of Mummy Research' in A.R. David, (ed.), *Science in Egyptology* (Manchester, 1986), pp. 211–217

Chapter 10 Cockburn, A., Barraco, A., Reyman, T.A. and Peck, W.H. 'Autopsy on Egyptian Mummy' in *Science*, Vol. 187 (1975), pp. 1155–1160

Curry, A., 'The Insects associated with the Manchester Mummies' in A.R. David, (ed.), *The Manchester Museum Mummy Project* (Manchester, 1979), pp. 113–117

Curry, A., Anfield, C., and Tapp, E., 'Electron Microscopy of the Manchester Mummies' in A.R. David, (ed.), *The Manchester Museum Mummy Project* (Manchester, 1979), pp. 103–111

Hufnagel, L., Communication in Palaeopathology Newsletter (1973)

Krypczyk, A. and Tapp, E., 'Immunohistochemistry and Electron Microscopy of Egyptian Mummies' in A.R. David, (ed.), *Science in Egyptology* (Manchester, 1986), pp. 361–365

Lewin, P., 'Paleo-electron Microscopy of Mummified Tissue' in *Nature*, Vol. 213 (1967), pp. 416–418

Shattock, S.G., 'Pathological Condition of the Aorta of King Menephtah' in *Proceedings of the Royal Society of Medicine*, Vol. 2 (1909), pp. 122–127

171

Tapp, E., 'Disease in the Manchester Mummies' in A.R. David, (ed.), *The Manchester Museum Mummy Project* (Manchester, 1979), pp. 95–102

Tapp, E., 'Disease in the Manchester Mummies: The Pathologist's Role' in David and Tapp (eds.), *Evidence Embalmed* (Manchester, 1984), pp. 78–95

Chapter 11   Blayds, J. *An Account of an Egyptian Mummy* (Leeds Philosophical and Literary Society, 1828) Republished Leeds, 1928

George, E.S., *An Account of an Egyptian Mummy* (Leeds Philosophical and Literary Society, 1828) Republished Leeds, 1928

Granville, A.B., 'An Essay on Egyptian Mummies, with Observations on the Art of Embalming amongst Ancient Egyptians' in *Philosophical Transactions of the Royal Society* (1825), pp. 269–316

Murray, M.A., *The Tomb of Two Brothers* (Manchester Museum Handbook, Manchester, 1910)

Ruffer, M.A., (1911) 'Histological Studies on Egyptian Mummies' in *Mem. Inst. Egypte*, Vol. 6, pp. 1–33

Sandison, A.T., 'Degenerative vascular disease in the Egyptian Mummy' in *Medical History*, Vol. 6, (1962), pp. 77–81

Sandison, A.T., 'The Egyptian Mummy Eye' in A.R. David, (ed.), *Science in Egyptology* (Manchester, 1986), pp. 7–9

Tapp, E., 'Disease in the Manchester Mummies' in A.R. David, (ed.), *The Manchester Museum Mummy Project* (Manchester, 1979), pp. 95–102

Tapp, E., 'The Unwrapping of a Mummy' in A.R. David, (ed.), *The Manchester Museum Mummy Project* (Manchester, 1979), pp. 83–94

Tapp, E., 'The Unwrapping of 1770' in A.R. David, (ed.), *Science in Egyptology* (Manchester, 1986), pp. 51–56

Tapp, E., Curry, A. and Anfield, C., 'Sand Pneumoconiosis in an Egyptian Mummy' in Brit. Med. J. (1975, Vol. 2) p. 276

Tapp, E., Stanworth, P. and Wildsmith, K., 'The Endoscope in Mummy Research' in A.R. David and E. Tapp (eds.), *Evidence Embalmed* (Manchester, 1984), pp. 65–77

Teale, T.B. and Hey, R., *An Account of an Egyptian Mummy* (Leeds Philosophical and Literary Society, 1828) Republished Leeds, 1928

Thompson, P., Lynch, P.G. and Tapp, E. 'Neuropathological Studies on the Manchester Mummies' in A.R. David, (ed.), *Science in Egyptology*, (Manchester, 1986), pp. 375–378

Chapter 12   Blundell, J., 'Observations on Transfusion of Blood by Dr Blundell' in *Lancet ii* (1828), pp. 321–324

Boyd, W.C. and Boyd, L.G., 'Group Specificity of Dried Muscle and Sliova' in *Journal of Immunology*, Vol. 26 (1934), pp. 489–494

Boyd, W.C. and Boyd, L.G., 'An Attempt to Determine the Blood Groups of Mummies' in *Proceedings of the Society of Experimental Biology*, Vol. 31 (1934), pp. 671–672

Boyd, W.C. and Boyd, L.G., 'Blood Grouping Tests on 300 Mummies' in *Journal of Immunology*, Vol. 32 (1937), pp. 307–319

Candela, P.B., 'Blood Group Reactions in Ancient Human Skeletons' in *American Journal of Physical Anthropology*, Vol. 21 (1936), pp. 429–432

Candela, P.B., 'Blood Group Determinations on Minnesota and New York Skeletal Material' in *American Journal of Physical Anthropology*, Vol. 23 (1937), pp. 71–78

Candela, P.B., 'Blood Group Determinations on the Bones of Thirty Aleutian Mummies' in *American Journal of Physical Anthropology*, Vol. 24 (1939), pp. 361–383

Jeffreys, A.J. et al, 'Positive Identification of an Immigrant Test Case using Human DNA Fingerprints' in *Nature*, Vol. 317 (1985), pp. 818–819

Katsunama, R. and Katsunama, S., 'On the Bone Marrow Cells of Man and Animal in the Stone Age of Japan' in *Proceedings of the Imperial Academy of Japan*, Vol. 5 (1929), pp. 388–389

Landsteiner, K., 'Uber Agglutinationserscheinungen normalen menschlichen' in *Blutes Wien Klin. Wochensche*, Vol. 14 (1901), pp. 1132–1134

Lengyel, I.A., in *Palaeoserology. Blood typing with the fluorescent antibody method* (Budapest Akademia Kaido, 1975)

Lippold, L.K., 'The Mixed Cell Agglutination Method for Typing Mummified Human Tissue' in *American Journal of Physical Anthropology*, Vol. 34 (1971), pp. 377–383

Stastny, P., 'HL-A Antigens in Mummified Pre-Columbian Tissues' in *Science*, Vol. 183 (1974), pp. 864–866

Chapter 13   David, A.R., (ed.), *Science in Egyptology* (Manchester, 1986): R.A.H. Neave, 'The Reconstruction of Skulls for Facial Reconstruction using Radiographic Techniques', pp. 329–336

Kollmann and Büchly, *Die Persistenz der Rassen und die Rekonstruktion der Physiognomie prähistorischer Schädel*. (Arch. f. Anth., 25. 1898)

Linney, A.D., Moss, J.P., Richards, R., et al., 'Use of 3-D Visualisation System in the Planning and Evaluation of Facial Surgery' in R.E. Herron, (ed.), *Proceedings of the Biometric Technology and Applications Meeting* (1991), pp. 190–199

Rhine, J.S. and Moore, C.E., 'Facial Reproduction Tables of Facial Thickness of American Caucasoids on Forensic Anthropology' in *Maxwell Museum Technical Series* 1. (New Mexico, 1983)

Stead, I.M., Bourke, J.B. and Brothwell, D.L., *Lindow Man: the Body in the Bog* (London, 1986), pp. 42–44

Further Reading

Asher, C., '500 years of History' in *Dental Practice*, Vol. 27, no. 7 (April 1989)

D'Athanasi, G., *Researches and Discoveries in Upper Egypt Made under the direction of Henry Salt Esq.* (1836)

Bernstein (1924), Thomsen (1930), quoted in Race, R.R. and Sanger, R., *Blood Groups in Man*, 6th ed., (Blackwell Scientific, Oxford)

Boorman, K.E. and Dodd, B.E., *Blood Grouping Serology*, 5th ed., (Churchill Livingstone, London, 1977)

Champollion, J.F., *Lettres a M. Le Duc de Blacas d'Aups . . . Relatives au Musee Royal Egyptien de Turin* (Paris, 1829)

Champollion, J.F., *Pantheon Egyptien* (Paris, 1823–5)

David, A.R. and Tapp, E., (eds.) *Evidence Embalmed* (Manchester, 1984)

Dawson, W.R., *Sir Grafton Elliot Smith* (London, 1938)

Dawson, W.R., and Gray, P.H.K., *Catalogue of the human remains in the Department of Egyptian Antiquities, British Museum* (London, 1968)

Gray, P.H.K., 'The Radiography of Mummies of Ancient Egyptians' in *Journal of Human Evolution*, Vol. 2 (1973), pp. 51–53

Harris, J.E. and Wente, E.F. (eds.), *An X-ray Atlas of the Royal Mummies* (Chicago, 1980)

Leek, F.F., 'The Practice of Dentistry in Ancient Egypt' in *Journal of Egyptian Archaeology*, Vol. 53 (1967), pp. 51–58

Leek, F.F., 'The Dental History of the Manchester Mummies' in A.R. David, (ed.), *The Manchester Mummy Project* (Manchester, 1979), pp. 65–77

Mourant, A.E. et al *Blood Groups and Diseases* (Oxford, 1978)

Murray, M.A., *My First Hundred Years* (London, 1963)

Ruffer, M.A., 'Histological Studies on Egyptian Mummies' in *Mem. Inst. Egypt*, Vol. 6, (1911), p. 3

Smith, N.J.D., 'Dental pathology in an Ancient Egyptian Population' in A.R. David, (ed.), *Science in Egyptology* (Manchester, 1986), pp. 43–48

Wilson, H., *Egyptian Food and Drink* (Shire Publications Ltd, Aylesbury, 1988)

Index